PHILIP'S

Cycle TOURS

Devon and Cornwall

Nick Cotton

First published in 2002 by
Philip's Ltd, a division of
Octopus Publishing Group Ltd
2-4 Heron Quays
London E14 4JP

First edition 2002

First impression 2002

Based on the original Ordnance Survey Cycle Tours series
first published by Philip's and Ordnance Survey®.

ISBN 0-540-08199-X

The route maps in this book are reproduced from
Ordnance Survey® Landranger® mapping.

Text and compilation copyright © Philip's Ltd 2002

Ordnance Survey®

This product includes mapping data licensed from Ordnance
Survey® with the permission of the Controller of Her Majesty's
Stationery Office. © Crown copyright 2002. All rights reserved.
Licence number 100011710

Photographic acknowledgements

John Bethell 7, 31 • Nick Cotton 55, 67, 73, 95, 103 top left,
107, 111 115 • Sylvia Cordaly 37 • Judy Todd 79, 99, 119, 123 •
Andy Williams: 13, 19

Contents

Abbreviations and symbols

Directions

L	left
R	right
LH	left-hand
RH	right-hand
SA	straight ahead or straight across
T-j	T-junction, a junction where you have to give way
X-roads	crossroads, a junction where you may or may not have to give way
'Placename 2'	words in quotation marks are those that appear on signposts; the numbers indicate distance in miles unless stated otherwise

Distance and grade

The number of drink bottles indicates the grade:

🍶 Easy

🍶🍶🍶 Moderate

🍶🍶🍶🍶🍶 Strenuous

The grade is based on the amount of climbing involved.

Refreshments

Pubs and teashops on or near the route are listed. The tankard 🍺 symbols indicate pubs particularly liked by the author.

Page diagrams

The page diagrams on the introductory pages show how the map pages have been laid out, how they overlap and if any inset maps have been used.

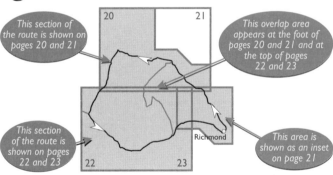

This section of the route is shown on pages 20 and 21

This overlap area appears at the foot of pages 20 and 21 and at the top of pages 22 and 23

This section of the route is shown on pages 22 and 23

This area is shown as an inset on page 21

Richmond

Cross-profiles

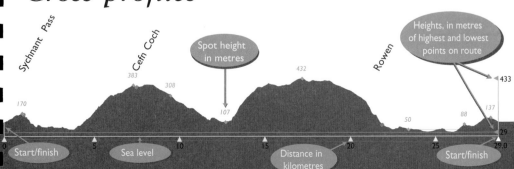

Sychnant Pass

Cefn Coch

Spot height in metres

Rowen

Heights, in metres of highest and lowest points on route

383

308

432

433

170

107

50

88

137

29

0

Start/finish

5

Sea level

10

15

Distance in kilometres

20

25

Start/finish

29.0

Legend to 1:50 000 maps

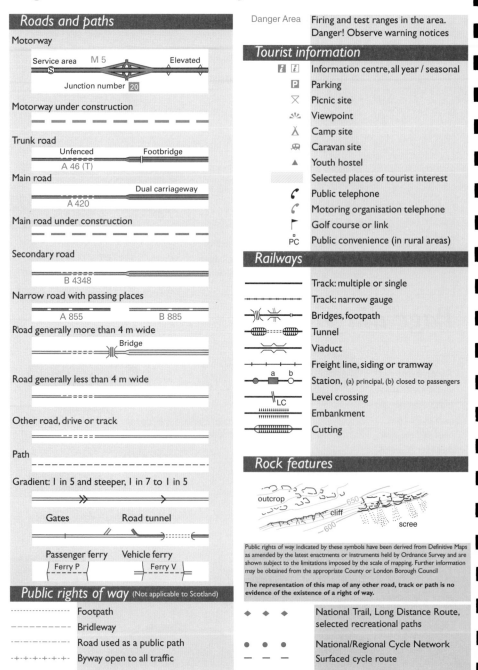

Roads and paths

Motorway

Service area   M 5   Elevated

Junction number **20**

Motorway under construction

Trunk road

Unfenced   Footbridge

A 46 (T)

Main road

Dual carriageway

A 420

Main road under construction

Secondary road

B 4348

Narrow road with passing places

A 855   B 885

Road generally more than 4 m wide

Bridge

Road generally less than 4 m wide

Other road, drive or track

Path

Gradient: 1 in 5 and steeper, 1 in 7 to 1 in 5

Gates   Road tunnel

Passenger ferry   Vehicle ferry

Ferry P   Ferry V

Public rights of way (Not applicable to Scotland)

Footpath
Bridleway
Road used as a public path
Byway open to all traffic

Danger Area | Firing and test ranges in the area. Danger! Observe warning notices

Tourist information

🅸 🅸	Information centre, all year / seasonal
🅿	Parking
✕	Picnic site
☼	Viewpoint
⅄	Camp site
⛺	Caravan site
▲	Youth hostel
	Selected places of tourist interest
☎	Public telephone
☎	Motoring organisation telephone
⌐	Golf course or link
PC	Public convenience (in rural areas)

Railways

Track: multiple or single
Track: narrow gauge
Bridges, footpath
Tunnel
Viaduct
Freight line, siding or tramway
Station, (a) principal, (b) closed to passengers
Level crossing
Embankment
Cutting

Rock features

outcrop cliff 650 600 scree

Public rights of way indicated by these symbols have been derived from Definitive Maps as amended by the latest enactments or instruments held by Ordnance Survey and are shown subject to the limitations imposed by the scale of mapping. Further information may be obtained from the appropriate County or London Borough Council

The representation of this map of any other road, track or path is no evidence of the existence of a right of way.

◆ ◆ ◆	National Trail, Long Distance Route, selected recreational paths
● ● ●	National/Regional Cycle Network
— — —	Surfaced cycle route

4

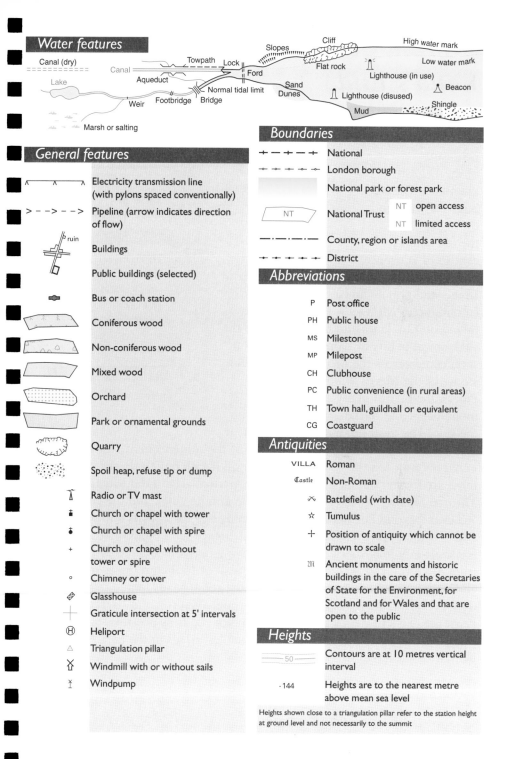

Water features

Canal (dry)
Canal
Aqueduct
Towpath
Lock
Ford
Weir
Footbridge
Bridge
Lake
Normal tidal limit
Marsh or salting
Slopes
Cliff
Flat rock
Sand
Dunes
Mud
High water mark
Low water mark
Lighthouse (in use)
Lighthouse (disused)
Beacon
Shingle

General features

Electricity transmission line (with pylons spaced conventionally)

> Pipeline (arrow indicates direction of flow)

ruin Buildings

Public buildings (selected)

Bus or coach station

Coniferous wood

Non-coniferous wood

Mixed wood

Orchard

Park or ornamental grounds

Quarry

Spoil heap, refuse tip or dump

Radio or TV mast

Church or chapel with tower

Church or chapel with spire

Church or chapel without tower or spire

Chimney or tower

Glasshouse

Graticule intersection at 5' intervals

Heliport

Triangulation pillar

Windmill with or without sails

Windpump

Boundaries

+ — + — + National

London borough

National park or forest park

NT National Trust NT open access NT limited access

County, region or islands area

District

Abbreviations

P Post office

PH Public house

MS Milestone

MP Milepost

CH Clubhouse

PC Public convenience (in rural areas)

TH Town hall, guildhall or equivalent

CG Coastguard

Antiquities

VILLA Roman

Castle Non-Roman

Battlefield (with date)

Tumulus

+ Position of antiquity which cannot be drawn to scale

Ancient monuments and historic buildings in the care of the Secretaries of State for the Environment, for Scotland and for Wales and that are open to the public

Heights

50 Contours are at 10 metres vertical interval

·144 Heights are to the nearest metre above mean sea level

Heights shown close to a triangulation pillar refer to the station height at ground level and not necessarily to the summit

5

From Penzance to Land's End

This is a trip around the westernmost peninsula of the English mainland. The ride hugs the seafront through the old fishing centres of Penzance,

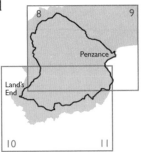

Newlyn and Mouse-hole. From the narrow streets and granite houses of Mousehole (pronounced 'Mowzel'), the route heads inland on tiny lanes and drops down to the subtropical plants of Lamorna Cove. You soon come across the Bronze Age standing stones of the Merry Maidens and the Pipers, the first of many ancient monuments and burial grounds passed on the ride. The most notable of these ancient remains are Carn Euny 3 km (2 miles) off the route from St Just and Lanyon Quoit (on the route). If you are taking all day to do the ride, there are further detours worth making, particularly to the Minack Theatre, an amphitheatre carved into the granite cliffs, and the church of St Levan beyond Porthcurno. Land's End is free for cyclists and walkers, and if you can cope with sharing the experience with the crowds, there are some fabulous views out to sea. Moving on, you come to St Just; from here, you can divert to Cape Cornwall or to the tin mines on the cliff's edge near Botallack. At Morvah, the route heads inland, passing over the bleak, windswept moorland through Madron and back to Penzance. This ride tries to use as few major roads as possible, but at the height of the holiday season, even the smallest roads in the area become busy with holiday traffic.

Start

Tourist Information Centre, Penzance

P Large car park next to the Tourist Information Centre

Distance and grade

51 km (32 miles)

Moderate/strenuous

Terrain

Three main climbs: 100 m (330 ft) south-west from Mousehole, 76 m (250 ft) west from Lamorna valley and 76 m (250 ft) southeast from Morvah

Nearest railway

Penzance

Penzance Newlyn Mousehole Castallack Lamorna Boskenna Treen Trethewey Trevescan Land's End Sennen

Places of interest

Penzance 1

A popular seaside resort, Penzance grew rich from the proceeds of fishing, the tin trade and smuggling. The fanciful Egyptian House in Chapel Street dates from 1820 and now houses the National Trust Information Centre. Morrab Gardens, near the sea front, contain subtropical plants.

Refreshments

Turks Head PH 🍺🍺 *and others in* Penzance
Ship PH 🍺🍺 *and others in* Mousehole
Lamorna Wink PH 🍺, Lamorna
Logan Rock PH 🍺🍺, Treen
Lots of choice at Land's End
Star Inn PH 🍺, *Miners Arms PH* 🍺
and others in St Just

The Merry Maidens and the Pipers 4/5

The stone circle of the Merry Maidens is said to be all that remains of the nineteen young ladies who dared to dance on the Sabbath. The pipers who played for them were also turned to granite and can be seen in nearby fields.

Carn Euny 3 km (2 miles) off the route from St Just 8

Carn Euny is an Iron Age village dating from the 1st century BC. There are traces of houses with living rooms and store rooms opening off a central courtyard. These remains are built around a 2nd-century 'fogou' or underground chamber, which is thought to have been used for storage, defence or religious ritual.

Land's End

Lanyon Quoit 10/11

Lanyon Quoit is one of the Penwith group of gallery graves (a Southern Irish form) and was once covered by a long mound or cairn. It is Neolithic, possibly dating from as early as 2000 BC.

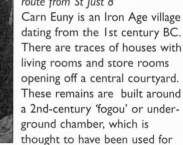

Kelynack   St Just   Botallack   Pendeen   Morrah   Madron

1 Follow the road along the seafront from the Tourist Information Centre 'Newlyn 1½, Mousehole 3½, Land's End 11'. At mini-roundabout by Beachfield Hotel bear L 'Newlyn 1, Mousehole 3. A3077 (B3315)'

2 Through Mousehole following the coast as closely as possible. At the end of the village, climb steeply uphill 'Lamorna'

➡ two pages

8 After 4 km (2½ miles) L on B3306 'St Just 3, Pendeen 6'

9 After 4 km (2½ miles), at T-j with A3071 L 'St Just ¼, Pendeen 3, Morvah 5, Zennor'. Through St Just following signs for Morvah

10 In Morvah, shortly after telephone box and church on left 1st R 'Madron 4, Penzance 5'

11 After 1½ km (1 mile), at T-j R 'Madron 3, Penzance 5'

12 After 5½ km (3½ miles), at roundabout SA 'Penzance Town Centre 2'. At mini-roundabout by West Cornwall Hospital SA

13 Just after passing the Fountain Tavern on the left, on a sharp LH bend with pedestrian area ahead R onto Clarence Street

14 At traffic lights at the end of Clarence Street L. Follow this street past the large, domed bank building

15 At traffic lights at the bottom of Market Jew Street, at the start of the one-way system, move into the RH lane 'Car Park, Tourist Information Centre' to return to start

PASSENGER FERRY FROM PENZANCE TO Isles of Scilly 2 hrs 40 mins (summer only)

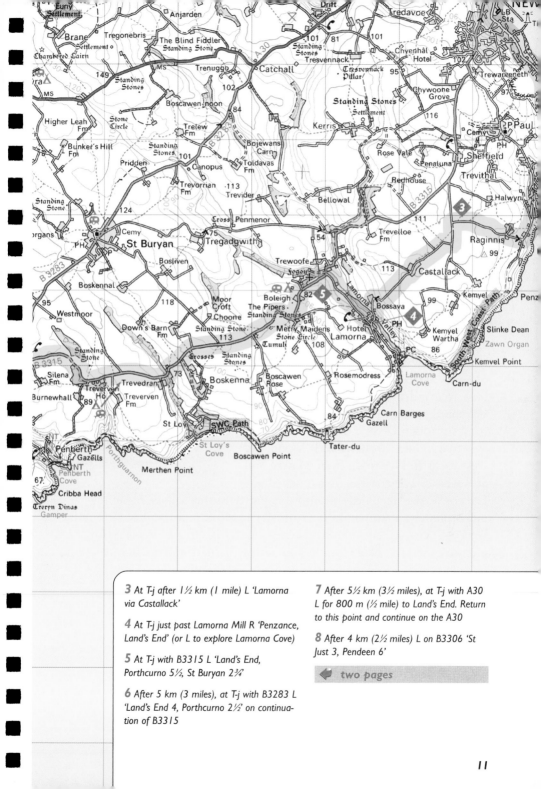

3 At T-j after 1½ km (1 mile) L 'Lamorna via Castallack'

4 At T-j just past Lamorna Mill R 'Penzance, Land's End' (or L to explore Lamorna Cove)

5 At T-j with B3315 L 'Land's End, Porthcurno 5½, St Buryan 2¾'

6 After 5 km (3 miles), at T-j with B3283 L 'Land's End 4, Porthcurno 2½ on continuation of B3315

7 After 5½ km (3½ miles), at T-j with A30 L for 800 m (½ mile) to Land's End. Return to this point and continue on the A30

8 After 4 km (2½ miles) L on B3306 'St Just 3, Pendeen 6'

◀ two pages

From Helston to Lizard Point, the southernmost point in mainland Britain

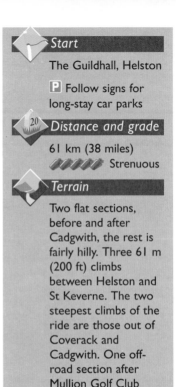
This ride is long enough, hard enough and surrounded by so many enticing diversions that it would be easy to spend two days doing it and exploring all the sights, villages and coastline along the way. A slightly complicated exit from the town, made necessary by hills, one-way systems and the wish to avoid busy roads, drops you close to the Flambard Village Theme Park. The ride passes through Gweek, with its Seal Sanctuary, then through lovely woodland westwards to Newtown-in-St Martin and St Keverne. The coast is first touched at Coverack, the steep descent into this pretty fishing village meaning, unfortunately, a steep climb out of it! The bleak moorland of Goonhilly Downs is crossed en route to the coast at Cadgwith, which is a tiny, picture-postcard village long-favoured by artists. Unfortunately, there is no coast-route for bikes from Cadgwith to Lizard Point, so you have to head inland before turning south to this most southerly point on mainland Britain. A few unavoidable miles on the A3083 must be covered before you turn off towards the temptations of Mullion. A short off-road section through a golf-course minimizes the time spent on the main road on your return to Helston.

14 Helston 15

16 Lizard Point 17

Helston Mellangoose Gweek Mawgan Newtown-in-St Martin Tregidden Tregowris St Keverne Coverack Penhallick Traboe Cross

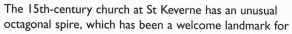
St Keverne 9

The 15th-century church at St Keverne has an unusual octagonal spire, which has been a welcome landmark for sailors for hundreds of years. Just a mile offshore, the treacherous Manacle Rocks have made shipwrecks a gruesome part of the village's history; over 400 victims are buried at the church.

Coverack 11

This charming old fishing village used to be a notorious smuggling centre. Wreckers lured unsuspecting vessels onto the Manacle Rocks to plunder their cargoes.

Goonhilly Downs 14

Goonhilly is a broad, windswept moor about seven square miles in area that was once covered by oak forest. Nowadays, the site is dominated by the British Telecom International Earth Station and there are eleven international dish aerials on site.

Cadgwith 16

Thatched cottages of green serpentine rock and boats beached on the shingle cove create this picturesque Cornish village.

Mullion Cove

Refreshments

Blue Anchor PH 🍺🍺 and others in Helston
Black Swan PH 🍺, Gweek
Old Court House Inn PH 🍺, Mawgan
Prince of Wales PH 🍺, Newtown-in-St Martin
Three Tuns PH, St Keverne
Paris Hotel PH, Coverack
Cadgwith Cove Inn PH 🍺, Cadgwith
Lots of choice at Lizard
Old Inn PH 🍺 and others in Mullion
Hazlephron Inn PH, Poldhu

Goonhilly Downs · Kuggar · Ruan Minor · Cadgwith · Lizard · Lizard Point · Mullion · Gunwalloe · Culdrose Airfield

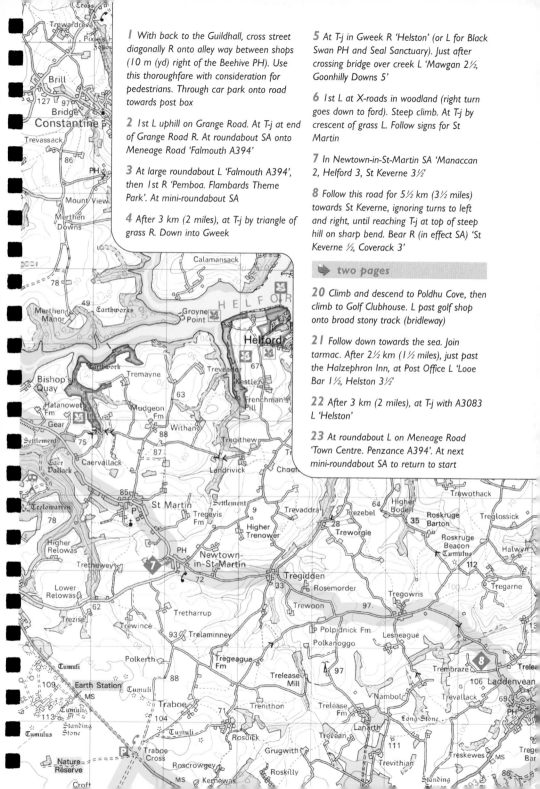

1 With back to the Guildhall, cross street diagonally R onto alley way between shops (10 m (yd) right of the Beehive PH). Use this thoroughfare with consideration for pedestrians. Through car park onto road towards post box

2 1st L uphill on Grange Road. At T-j at end of Grange Road R. At roundabout SA onto Meneage Road 'Falmouth A394'

3 At large roundabout L 'Falmouth A394', then 1st R 'Pemboa. Flambards Theme Park'. At mini-roundabout SA

4 After 3 km (2 miles), at T-j by triangle of grass R. Down into Gweek

5 At T-j in Gweek R 'Helston' (or L for Black Swan PH and Seal Sanctuary). Just after crossing bridge over creek L 'Mawgan 2½, Goonhilly Downs 5'

6 1st L at X-roads in woodland (right turn goes down to ford). Steep climb. At T-j by crescent of grass L. Follow signs for St Martin

7 In Newtown-in-St-Martin SA 'Manaccan 2, Helford 3, St Keverne 3½'

8 Follow this road for 5½ km (3½ miles) towards St Keverne, ignoring turns to left and right, until reaching T-j at top of steep hill on sharp bend. Bear R (in effect SA) 'St Keverne ½, Coverack 3'

➡ **two pages**

20 Climb and descend to Poldhu Cove, then climb to Golf Clubhouse. L past golf shop onto broad stony track (bridleway)

21 Follow down towards the sea. Join tarmac. After 2½ km (1½ miles), just past the Halzephron Inn, at Post Office L 'Looe Bar 1½, Helston 3½'

22 After 3 km (2 miles), at T-j with A3083 L 'Helston'

23 At roundabout L on Meneage Road 'Town Centre. Penzance A394'. At next mini-roundabout SA to return to start

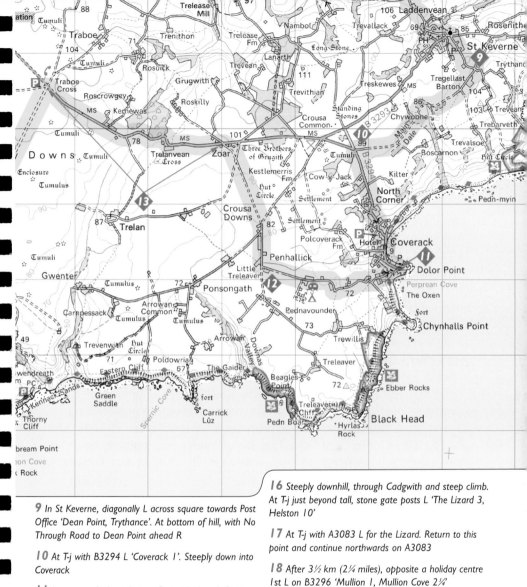

9 In St Keverne, diagonally L across square towards Post Office 'Dean Point, Trythance'. At bottom of hill, with No Through Road to Dean Point ahead R

10 At T-j with B3294 L 'Coverack 1'. Steeply down into Coverack

11 Just past telephone box in Coverack sharply R up steep hill

12 At T-j with Give Way sign R 'Helston 10'

13 At T-j with B3293 L (no sign). After 3 km (2 miles), 1st L at X-roads 'Kennack Sands 3, Cadgwith 4'

14 After 5 km (3 miles) across Goonhilly Downs, in Kuggar R 'Ruan Minor 1, Cadgwith 1¾'

15 At X-roads L 'Ruan Minor, Cadgwith ¾'

16 Steeply downhill, through Cadgwith and steep climb. At T-j just beyond tall, stone gate posts L 'The Lizard 3, Helston 10'

17 At T-j with A3083 L for the Lizard. Return to this point and continue northwards on A3083

18 After 3½ km (2¼ miles), opposite a holiday centre 1st L on B3296 'Mullion 1, Mullion Cove 2¼'

19 Through Mullion on one-way system. At T-j by The Cottage Restaurant R 'Poldhu Cove 1, Helston 9' (or L to explore Mullion Cove). At next T-j L 'Poldhu Cove 1, Cury 2¼'

20 Climb and descend to Poldhu Cove, then climb to Golf Clubhouse. L past golf shop onto broad stony track (bridleway)

◀ **two pages**

3 ▸ North, then west from Falmouth via Mylor, returning via Helford River

You can start this ride on a boat: a short ferry ride drops you at Flushing on the Mylor peninsula. If you do not feel up to this, however, a road alternative is described. The hills climbed at the start of the ride give you fabulous views over Carrick Roads, the unusual name for the stretch of water lying between Falmouth and Truro. From Perranarworthal, the route heads inland through parts of Cornwall, little touched by the mining that has affected so much of the interior of the county. Should you be feeling adventurous, you may wish to explore underground at the Poldark Mine and Heritage Complex at Wendron. If you prefer horticulture, however, there are two magnificent, exotic gardens at Glendurgan and Trebah, between Porth Navas and Mawnan Smith. As you head north back towards Falmouth, views of the sea open up.

Start

Tourist Information Centre, Falmouth

P Long-stay car park

Distance and grade

46 km (29 miles)

Moderate/strenuous

Terrain

All hilly! 6 climbs of between 61 and 51 m (200 and 170 ft) and several shorter ones

Nearest railway

Falmouth

Refreshments

Lots of choice in Falmouth *Lemon Arms PH* 🍴, Mylor Bridge *Pandora Inn PH* 🍴🍴, *just off the route in* Restronguet Passage *Star Inn PH*, Porkellis *Queens Arms PH*, Constantine *Red Lion PH* 🍴🍴, Mawnan Smith

Falmouth · Flushing · Mylor Churchtown · Mylor Bridge · Angarrick · Perran Wharf · Perranarworthal · Tubbon Hill · Stithians · Tregolls · Herniss · Carnkie · Porkellis

Falmouth /

Falmouth stands at the entrance to the Carrick Roads, a beautiful stretch of water formed by the merging of seven river estuaries. It has a huge natural harbour on one side. Local smuggling has its monument in the King's Pipe, a brick chimney on the slope leading down to Custom House Quay, which was used for burning illegally imported tobacco.

Pendennis Castle, Falmouth /

Built by Henry VIII in 1544-46, Pendennis Castle was one of a chain of castles constructed to deter a French invasion. It has a circular keep with drawbridge, portcullis, spyholes and spiral staircase; there are superb views of the surrounding area.

The Poldark Mine and Heritage Complex, Wendron /4

There are easy and difficult underground routes to explore, as well as seeing Poldark village and the Museum Chambers.

Constantine /9

One of Cornwall's main quarrying areas, Constantine provided the granite for London's original Waterloo Bridge. Many buildings in the village are made of granite. In a field just north of

The Helford Passage from above Helford village looking towards Porth Navas

the village is Piskey Hall, an ancient underground passage with granite walls known as a 'fogou', the Cornish word for cave. It was originally part of a prehistoric fortification.

Glendurgan Gardens (south of Mawnan Smith) 23

A small valley descending to the Helford Passage has been turned into an oasis of exotic flowers, trees and shrubs. The adjoining Trebah Gardens are also worth visiting.

Trenear   Trussall   Brill   Constantine Ponjeravah   Porth Navas   Mawnan Smith   Maenporth   Swanpool Beach

1 With back to Tourist Information Centre, cross to other side of the square. R following the one-way system downhill to the quay for the ferry to Flushing. (1st pier on left, pay on boat)

2 From Flushing Pier L 'Mylor Church. Mylor Bridge'. Follow signs for Mylor Church

3 On fast descent towards the harbour, slow down when you see stone cross by the church, L onto Public Footpath

4 At end of Church Road R 'Mylor Bridge ¼, Truro 8¼'. At T-j with Lemon Hill R 'Restronguet 1¼, Truro 9'. (Road and Ferry routes join)

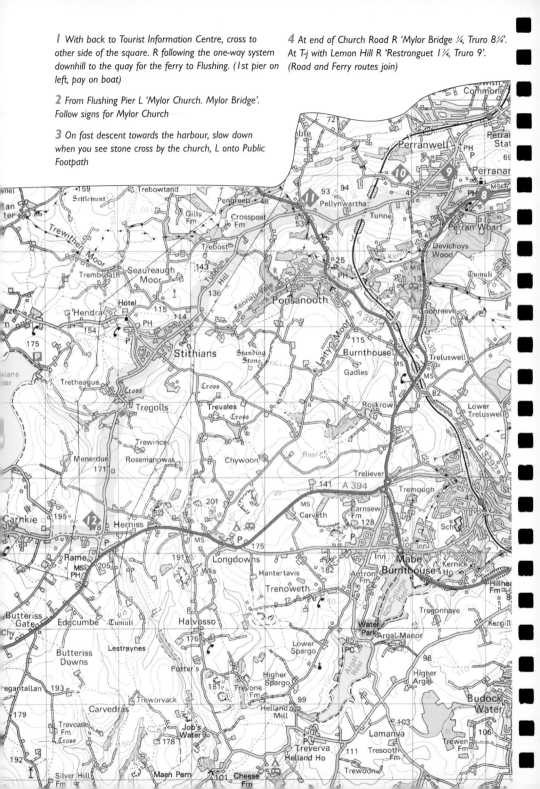

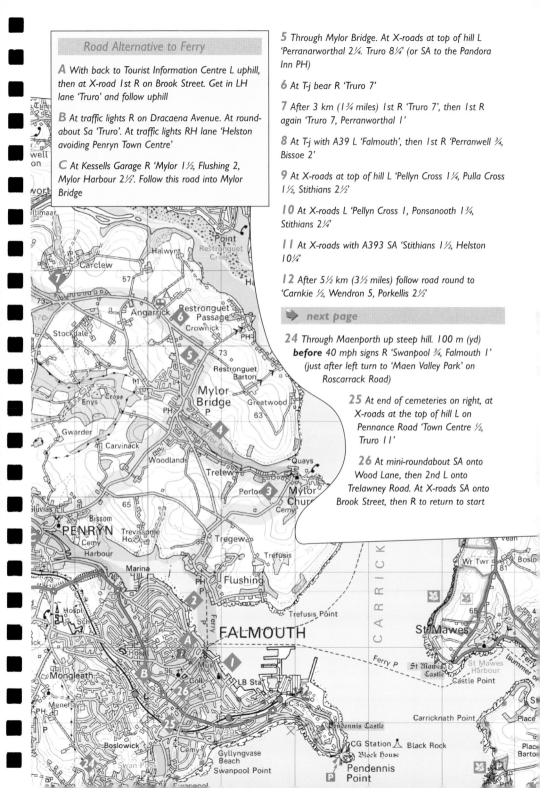

next page

Road Alternative to Ferry

A With back to Tourist Information Centre L uphill, then at X-road 1st R on Brook Street. Get in LH lane 'Truro' and follow uphill

B At traffic lights R on Dracaena Avenue. At round-about Sa 'Truro'. At traffic lights RH lane 'Helston avoiding Penryn Town Centre'

C At Kessells Garage R 'Mylor 1½, Flushing 2, Mylor Harbour 2½'. Follow this road into Mylor Bridge

5 Through Mylor Bridge. At X-roads at top of hill L 'Perranarworthal 2¼. Truro 8¼' (or SA to the Pandora Inn PH)

6 At T-j bear R 'Truro 7'

7 After 3 km (1¾ miles) 1st R 'Truro 7', then 1st R again 'Truro 7, Perranwothal 1'

8 At T-j with A39 L 'Falmouth', then 1st R 'Perranwell ¾, Bissoe 2'

9 At X-roads at top of hill L 'Pellyn Cross 1¼, Pulla Cross 1½, Stithians 2½'

10 At X-roads L 'Pellyn Cross 1, Ponsanooth 1¾, Stithians 2¼'

11 At X-roads with A393 SA 'Stithians 1½, Helston 10¼'

12 After 5½ km (3½ miles) follow road round to 'Carnkie ½, Wendron 5, Porkellis 2½'

24 Through Maenporth up steep hill. 100 m (yd) **before** 40 mph signs R 'Swanpool ¾, Falmouth 1' (just after left turn to 'Maen Valley Park' on Roscarrack Road)

25 At end of cemeteries on right, at X-roads at the top of hill L on Pennance Road 'Town Centre ½, Truro 11'

26 At mini-roundabout SA onto Wood Lane, then 2nd L onto Trelawney Road. At X-roads SA onto Brook Street, then R to return to start

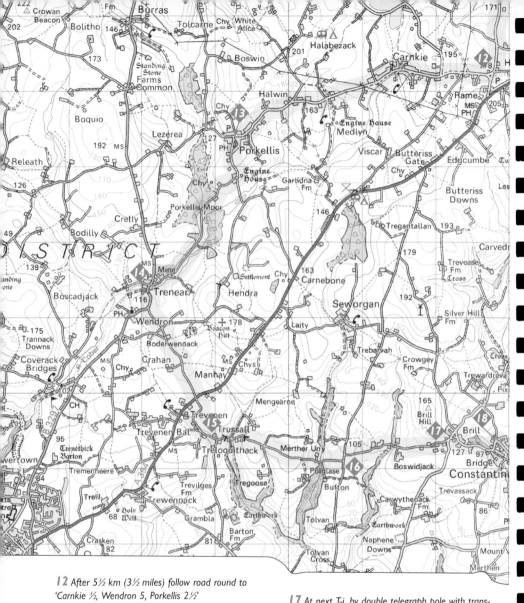

12 After 5½ km (3½ miles) follow road round to 'Carnkie ½, Wendron 5, Porkellis 2½'

13 In Porkellis L at Star Inn PH 'Wendron 2, Helston 4'

14 At T-j with B3297 L 'Helston 3'. After 200 m (yd), on RH bend L 'Trevenen 1½, Gweek 3½'

15 At X-roads with with A394 SA 'Gweek 2¾'. 1st L by house with letter box in wall 'Treloquithack ¼, Constantine 3'

16 At T-j L then R (NS)

17 At next T-j, by double telegraph pole with transformer L, then R.. At T-j by vicarage after 100 m (yd) R

18 At next T-j, opposite row of bungalows R 'Constantine ¼'

19 Through Constantine, down hill and over bridge. 1st R 'Porth Navas 1¼'

20 Follow signs for 'Helford Passage' and 'Mawnan Smith'

21 Just after crossing bridge over stream at bottom of hill L

22 At T-j at top R (NS), then at T-j at junction of penwarne Road and Sampys Hill R

23 In Mawnan Smith L at the Red Lion PH on Carwinion Road

24 Through Maenporth up steep hill. 100 m (yd) **before** 40 mph signs R 'Swanpool ¾, Falmouth 1' (just after left turn to 'Maen Valley Park' on Roscarrack Road)

two pages

From Truro on small lanes around the Tresillian, Fal and Truro rivers

The Fal Estuary separates two contrasting landscapes: to the west lie the ugly scars of centuries of tin mining, to the east is the delightful Roseland Peninsula, almost entirely untouched and

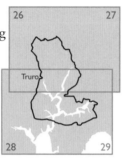

unspoilt. It is through the latter that this ride weaves its way. It avoids the busy roads leading out of Truro by following tiny, wooded lanes up the valley of the River Allen north through Idless, Gwarnick and Treworgan, crossing the A3076 at St Erme. The A39 is similarly avoided by crossing it at Tresillian, leading you into the peaceful lanes around the estate of Tregothnan, which, unfortunately, is not open to the public. The thickly wooded lanes eventually take you to the bridge over the Fal at Ruan Lanihorne. More tiny lanes through Trelonk and Treworga take you past the splendid pub at Philleigh. On reaching the B3289, you can divert to the wonderful churchyard at St Just in Roseland, full of exotic plants and trees, or you can push on to the King Harry Ferry and the Trelissick Gardens on the other side of the estuary. The route back to Truro avoids the A39 by passing through Playing Place and Calenick.

Start

Tourist Information Centre, Truro

P Long-stay car park on the B3284 Perranporth Road

Distance and grade

40 km (25 miles)

Moderate

Terrain

Three hills of 76 m (250 ft): north from Truro, south from Tresillian and southwest from Ruan Lanihorne

Nearest railway

Truro

Truro Idless Gwarnick Lanner Barton Treworgan St Erme Tresillian Tregerrick Merther Lane St Michael Penkevil

Truro 1

The three great spires of Truro Cathedral rise dramatically above a cluster of narrow streets filled with elegant Georgian houses. The cathedral was only built at the beginning of this century to a design inspired by medieval architecture. The County Museum has impressive displays of Cornwall's history.

Refreshments

Lots of choice in Truro
The Wheel PH ✦✦, *Tresillian*
Kings Head PH, Ruan Lanihorne
Roseland PH ✦✦, *Philleigh*

St Michael Penkevil 9

The church at St Michael Penkevil has interesting Pre-Raphaelite windows.

The Malpas Ferry *(off the route before St Michael Penkevil) 9*
This ferry used to be the main route into Truro from the east and carried horse-drawn vehicles as well as passengers. Legend says that Tristan and Isolde used the ferry on their ill-fated journey to Tintagel, and that the name of Malpas – from the French for bad passage – derives from the tragedy of their love affair.

Veryan *(2½ km (1½ miles) off the route near Treworga) 11*
Lying in a beautiful, wooded valley, this quiet village is famous for its round 'Devil-proof' houses. The houses, built in the early 19th century, are white-washed with conical thatched roofs and topped with a cross. Locals believed that Satan could not hide in a house without corners.

St Just in Roseland *(5 km (3 miles) south of the route at King Harry Ferry) 12*
This tiny hamlet lies tucked away up a creek of the Carrick Roads. It has one of the most beautiful churchyards in the country, full of luxuriant and exotic shrubs and trees.

Trelissick Garden 13

This large garden is lovely in all seasons. It has rare shrubs and plants, as well as an extensive park with woods and farmland. There are beautiful views over the Fal Estuary and Falmouth harbour.

Lamorran   Ruan Lanihorne   Treworga   Philleigh   Trelissick   Penelewey   Playing Place   Calenick

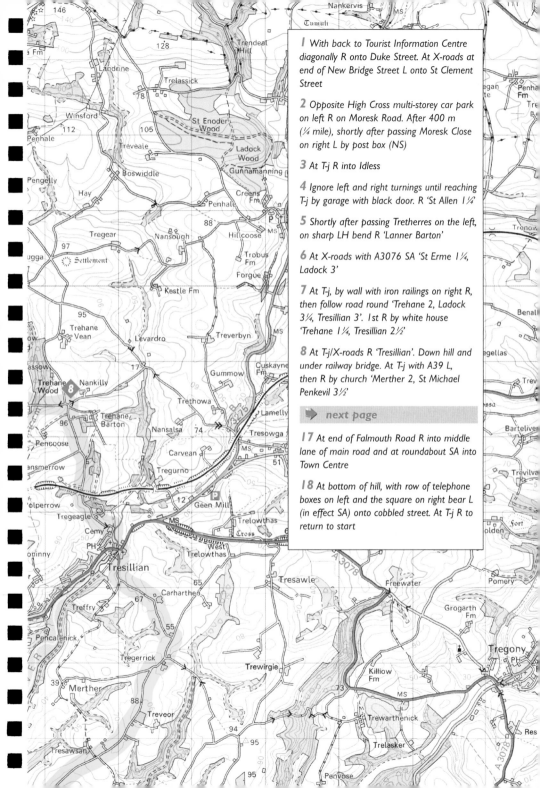

1 With back to Tourist Information Centre diagonally R onto Duke Street. At X-roads at end of New Bridge Street L onto St Clement Street

2 Opposite High Cross multi-storey car park on left R on Moresk Road. After 400 m (¼ mile), shortly after passing Moresk Close on right L by post box (NS)

3 At T-j R into Idless

4 Ignore left and right turnings until reaching T-j by garage with black door. R 'St Allen 1¼'

5 Shortly after passing Tretherres on the left, on sharp LH bend R 'Lanner Barton'

6 At X-roads with A3076 SA 'St Erme 1¼, Ladock 3'

7 At T-j, by wall with iron railings on right R, then follow road round 'Trehane 2, Ladock 3¼, Tresillian 3'. 1st R by white house 'Trehane 1¼, Tresillian 2½'

8 At T-j/X-roads R 'Tresillian'. Down hill and under railway bridge. At T-j with A39 L, then R by church 'Merther 2, St Michael Penkevil 3½'

➡ *next page*

17 At end of Falmouth Road R into middle lane of main road and at roundabout SA into Town Centre

18 At bottom of hill, with row of telephone boxes on left and the square on right bear L (in effect SA) onto cobbled street. At T-j R to return to start

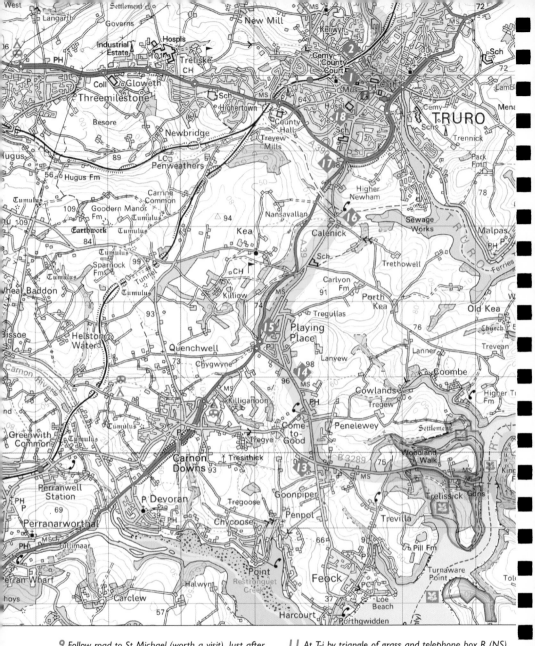

9 *Follow road to St Michael (worth a visit). Just after passing a right turn to 'Malpas ferry', with No Through Road ahead L 'Lamorran 1¾, Ruan Lanihorne 3'*

10 *After 3 km (2 miles), in wood 1st R 'Ruan Lanihorne 1'. At T-j R 'Ruan High Lanes 2', then 1st R 'Trethella ¼, Trelonk ¾'*

11 *At T-j by triangle of grass and telephone box R (NS). At next T-j R 'Philleigh, King Harry'*

12 *Through Philleigh. At T-j with B3289 R 'King Harry Ferry ½, Truro via Ferry 5½, Falmouth 11'*

13 *At T-j with B3289 R 'Truro 3½, Falmouth 7¼'*

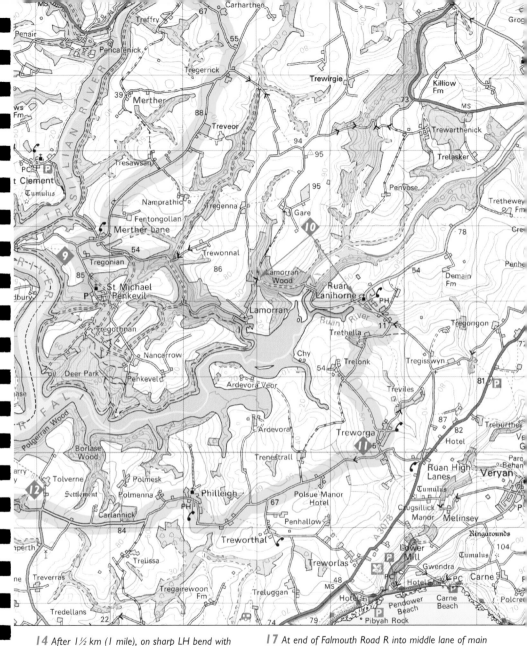

14 After 1½ km (1 mile), on sharp LH bend with chevrons R on Halvarras Road

15 At end of Holywell Road, just **before** roundabout R on Old Coach Road 'Porth Kea 1¼, Old Kea 2½'

16 In Calenick R over bridge towards telephone box 'No cars except access'

17 At end of Falmouth Road R into middle lane of main road and at roundabout SA into Town Centre

18 At bottom of hill, with row of telephone boxes on left and the square on right bear L (in effect SA) onto cobbled street. At T-j R to return to start

29

Southeast along the Camel Trail from Wadebridge and north to Port Isaac

The ride uses the eastern, less-frequented section of the Camel Trail, following the River Camel for 19 km (12 miles) through delightful woodland. After so long on a

wonderful gradient (you have climbed a mere 48 m (160 ft) so far), it is a shock to face the outrageous Cornish lanes: in the first 2½ km (1½ miles) after the end of the cycle path you have to climb 70 m (230 ft). The lanes are quiet, however, and the villages of St Tudy and St Teath are attractive in the solid way typical of villages near the Cornish coast. One of the loveliest stretches comes after St Teath: a 76 m (250 ft) climb leaves you on top of a hill with magnificent views out to sea. You soon gain speed as you zip down the hill into the pretty coastal villages of Portgaverne and Port Isaac. The latter is very popular in the holiday season. A reasonably tough hill awaits you as you leave Port Isaac, only the insane are expected to stay on their bikes! The ride continues westwards to the wide, sandy beach of Polzeath, which provides some of the best surfing in Cornwall. Further south is Rock, burial place of Sir John Betjeman. There are more superb views of the estuary before 3 km (2 miles) on slightly busier roads bring you back to Wadebridge.

 Start

Tourist Information Centre, Wadebridge

P Follow signs

 Distance and grade

53 km (33 miles)
Moderate (the Camel Trail section is ideal for the laziest cyclist)

Terrain

Four main climbs: 70 m (230 ft) from the end of the Camel Trail to St Tudy, 106 m (350 ft) to the ridge west of St Teath, a very steep 100 m (330 ft) south from Port Isaac and 70 m (230 ft) between Polzeath and Rock

 Nearest railway

Bodmin Parkway, 13 km (8 miles) east of the Camel Trail

Wadebridge · Boscarne · Dunmere · Hellandbridge · Poley's Bridge · St Tudy · St Teath

Port Isaac 14

White-painted and slate-hung cottages stand in tiers above the harbour of Port Isaac. They are interlaced with narrow passages called 'drangs', one of which is known as 'Squeeze-Belly Alley'. A stream runs down through the village to the harbour, where fishing boats unload their catches of lobsters and crabs.

The Carnel estuary

St Endellion *(just off the route)* 15

The church at St Endellion is beautiful.

Rock 20

Rock is named after an outcrop of dark greenstone that is known locally as Blacktor or Black Rock. The wind-blown, shifting sand in the estuary has often buried parts of the coastline. For six centuries, a ferryboat called the Blacktor has plied between Rock and Padstow. It started in 1337 with a rowboat, progressed to a sailboat, and now the Blacktor is a motor launch operated by Padstow Harbour commissioners. Sir John Betjeman is buried in St Enodoc Churchyard.

Refreshments

Molesworth Arms PH 🍺 *and others in* Wadebridge
Cornish Arms PH, St Tudy
White Hart PH 🍺, *tea shop,* St Teath
Port Gaverne Hotel PH, Portgaverne
Golden Lion PH 🍺 *and others in* Port Isaac
Pentire Rocks PH 🍺 *and others in* Polzeath
Lots of choice in Rock
Malsters Arms PH 🍺🍺, *just off the route*
in Chapel Amble

Portgaverne
Port Isaac
Trelights
Polzeath
Trebetherick
Porthilly
Trewornan

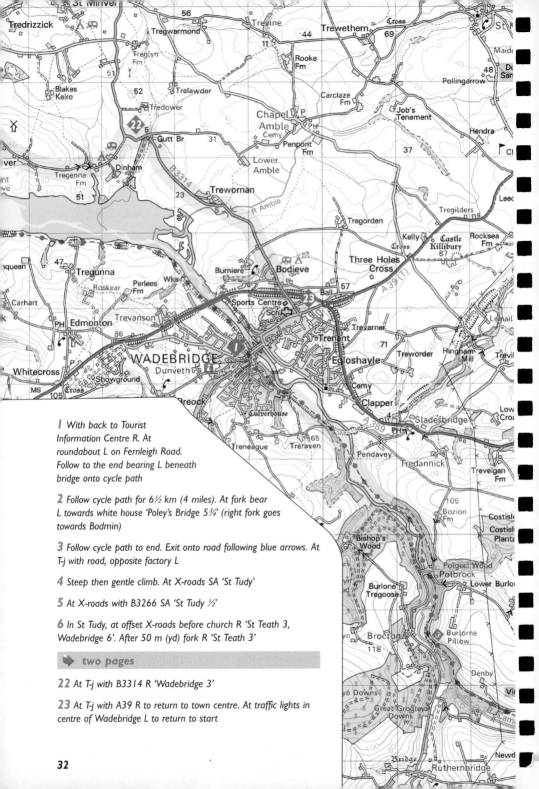

1 With back to Tourist Information Centre R. At roundabout L on Fernleigh Road. Follow to the end bearing L beneath bridge onto cycle path

2 Follow cycle path for 6½ km (4 miles). At fork bear L towards white house 'Poley's Bridge 5¾' (right fork goes towards Bodmin)

3 Follow cycle path to end. Exit onto road following blue arrows. At T-j with road, opposite factory L

4 Steep then gentle climb. At X-roads SA 'St Tudy'

5 At X-roads with B3266 SA 'St Tudy ½'

6 In St Tudy, at offset X-roads before church R 'St Teath 3, Wadebridge 6'. After 50 m (yd) fork R 'St Teath 3'

➡ **two pages**

22 At T-j with B3314 R 'Wadebridge 3'

23 At T-j with A39 R to return to town centre. At traffic lights in centre of Wadebridge L to return to start

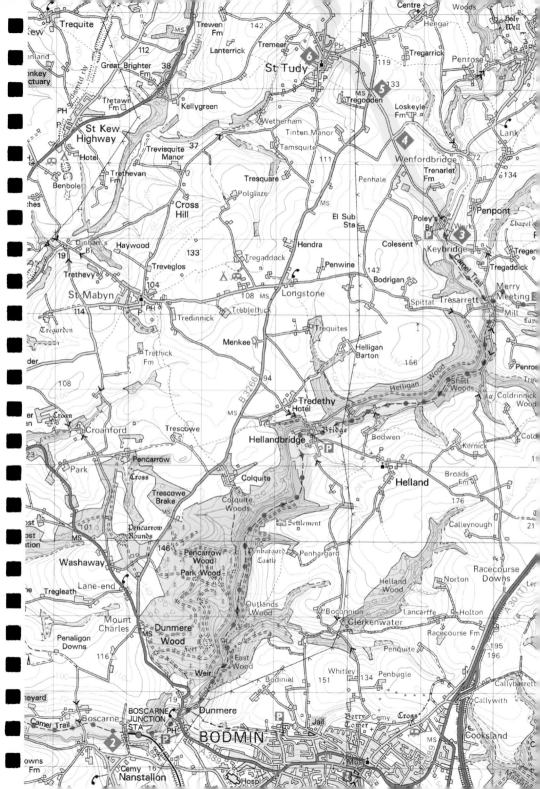

6 In St Tudy, at offset X-roads before church R 'St Teath 3, Wadebridge 6'. After 50 m (yd) fork R 'St Teath 3'

7 At X-roads SA (NS)

8 Take care. At T-j with A39 R, then L 'St Teath, Delabole'

9 At T-j by Paradise Park R 'St Teath ¼'

10 At clocktower in St Teath L, then after 50 m (yd) 1st L by Tregarthen B&B

11 At T-j by triangle of grass R 'Polzeath 7, Port Isaac 3½, Delabole 2¾, Port Gaverne 2½'

12 At X-roads with B3314 SA 'Port Gaverne 2'

13 Lovely coastal views. Down into, and up away from, Portgaverne. On sharp LH bend in Port Isaac, by phone box bear R (in effect SA) onto Back Hill '16% Unsuitable for caravans'

14 Steeply down. At T-j L to continue downhill. Through Port Isaac and up horribly steep hill. At T-j R 'Port Quin 1½, Wadebridge 7¼, Trelights ½'

15 Follow signs for Wadebridge through Trelights. At T-j with B3314 R 'Wadebridge 5¾'

16 After 1 km (¾ mile) 1st R 'Portquin 1½, Polzeath 2¼'

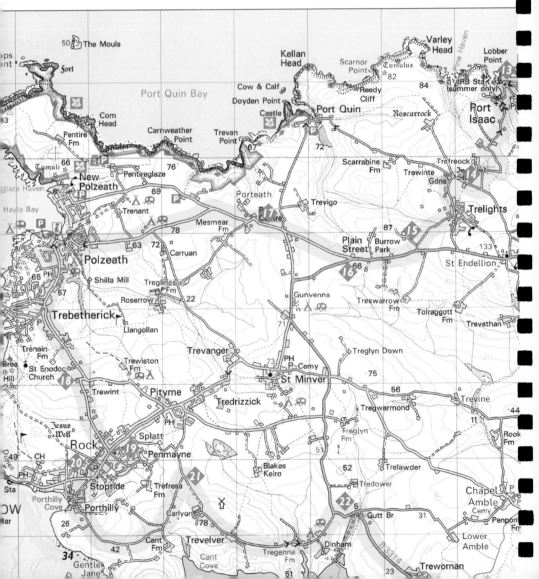

34

17 At T-j R 'Polzeath 2'

18 Through Polzeath, up steep then gentle hill. Descend, then climb a second hill. 2½ km (1½ miles) after leaving centre of Polzeath R at top of hill 'Rock 1½'

19 At X-roads at end of Trewint Lane, opposite Clock Garage R

20 After 400 m (¼ mile), just after white house with blue shutters on left (opposite wooden fence with a hedge above) L onto small lane 'Porthilly'

21 Fine views over estuary. 1st R by telegraph pole carrying three lines

22 At T-j with B3314 R 'Wadebridge 3'

three pages

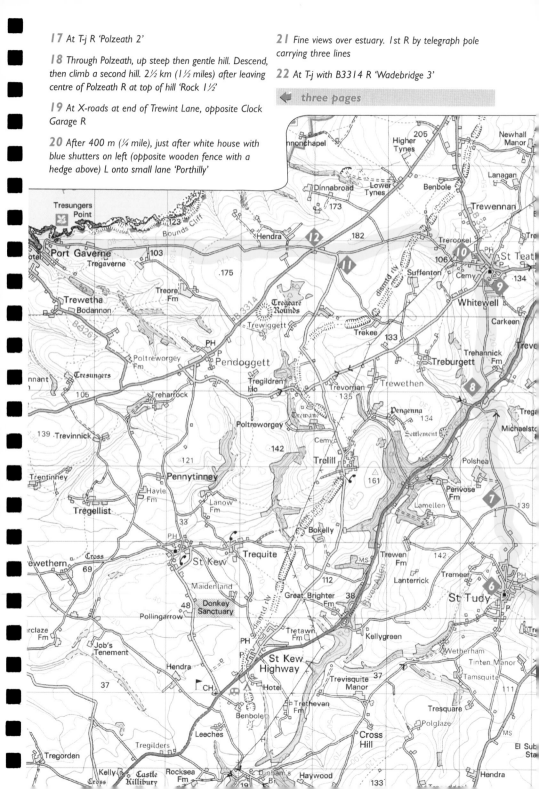

On the Camel Trail west from Wadebridge to Padstow and on to Mawgan Porth

Start
Tourist Information Centre, Wadebridge

P Follow signs

Distance and grade
48 km (30 miles)
Moderate

Terrain
Two climbs of 61 m (200 ft), west from Padstow and south from Penrose. One longer climb from Mawgan Porth south-east to cross the A39

Nearest railway
Bodmin Parkway, 13 km (8 miles) east of Ruthernbridge

This ride makes use of the Camel Trail, perhaps the most famous and well-loved cycle trail in the country. It certainly has much to commend it, with an excellent surface and lovely estuary views. Its popularity means that it is a ride to be enjoyed slowly, however, as there are often families with young children wobbling their way along the trail. Padstow's charms are best appreciated out of season as the place can get very busy. The ride heads inland towards St Merryn, then cuts south on small lanes past a collection of ugly MOD antennae at St Eval. It drops down to the sea at Mawgan Porth. From here on, the ride really comes into its own, climbing the ridge above the thickly wooded Vale of Lanherne, from which you must divert if you wish to see the lovely

church at St Mawgan. Soon after crossing the A39, you plunge into a network of tiny lanes that follows a stream valley through hidden hamlets to Ruthernbridge and then through forest to the bridge at Polbrock. Here, you rejoin the Camel Trail and go northwards back to Padstow.

Wadebridge   Padstow   Windmill St Merryn   Penrose   Trenance

Wadebridge 1

The centrepiece of this small market town is a fine medieval bridge that crosses the River Camel to Egloshayle. It was built by the vicar of Egloshayle in 1485 because he deemed the ferry crossing too dangerous for his parishioners.

Padstow harbour

Padstow 2

One of north Cornwall's oldest fishing towns, Padstow's days as an export port ended in the mid-19th century when the Camel estuary silted up. St Petroc's Church dates from the 6th century when St Petroc came here from Ireland to found a monastery. Padstow's tropical bird and butterfly gardens include a heated, walk-in tropical house, which enables visitors to see free-flying exotic birds at close quarters.

Prideaux Place 2

Prideaux Place was built in 1585 on the site of a monastic grange belonging to Bodmin Priory. There is an underground passage linking it with Abbey House on Padstow Harbour.

St Merryn 6

In the church at St Merryn is a beautiful, 14th-century font.

St Mawgan 14/15

The churchyard at St Mawgan contains a remarkable lantern cross of 1420, several fine Celtic crosses and a wooden memorial shaped like the stern of a boat; this is dedicated to nine men and a boy who froze to death in their lifeboat after their ship was wrecked in 1846.

Lanvean   Tregamere   Rosenannon   Ruthernbridge   Polbrock

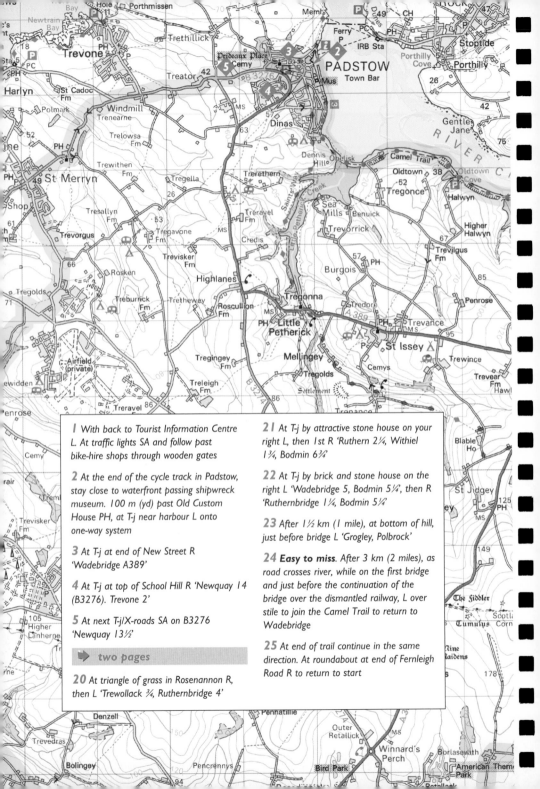

1 With back to Tourist Information Centre L. At traffic lights SA and follow past bike-hire shops through wooden gates

2 At the end of the cycle track in Padstow, stay close to waterfront passing shipwreck museum. 100 m (yd) past Old Custom House PH, at T-j near harbour L onto one-way system

3 At T-j at end of New Street R 'Wadebridge A389'

4 At T-j at top of School Hill R 'Newquay 14 (B3276). Trevone 2'

5 At next T-j/X-roads SA on B3276 'Newquay 13½'

➥ two pages

20 At triangle of grass in Rosenannon R, then L 'Trewollack ¾, Ruthernbridge 4'

21 At T-j by attractive stone house on your right L, then 1st R 'Ruthern 2¼, Withiel 1¾, Bodmin 6¾'

22 At T-j by brick and stone house on the right L 'Wadebridge 5, Bodmin 5¼', then R 'Ruthernbridge 1¼, Bodmin 5¼'

23 After 1½ km (1 mile), at bottom of hill, just before bridge L 'Grogley, Polbrock'

24 **Easy to miss**. After 3 km (2 miles), as road crosses river, while on the first bridge and just before the continuation of the bridge over the dismantled railway, L over stile to join the Camel Trail to return to Wadebridge

25 At end of trail continue in the same direction. At roundabout at end of Fernleigh Road R to return to start

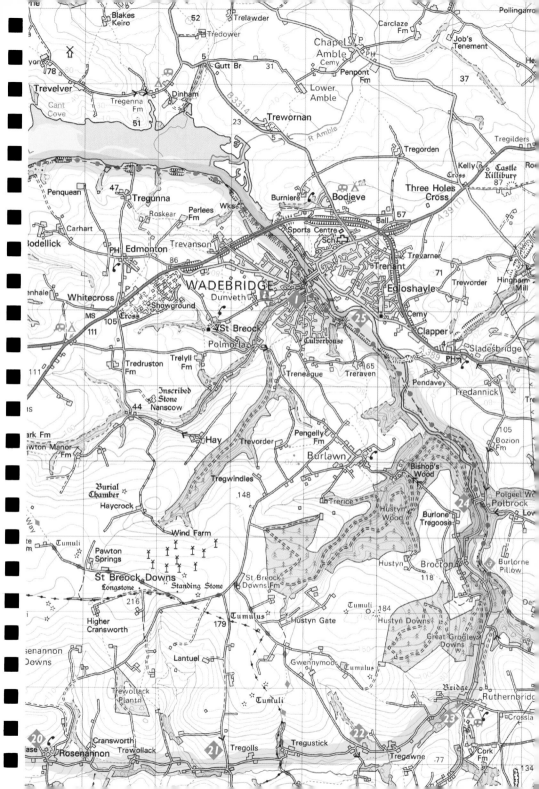

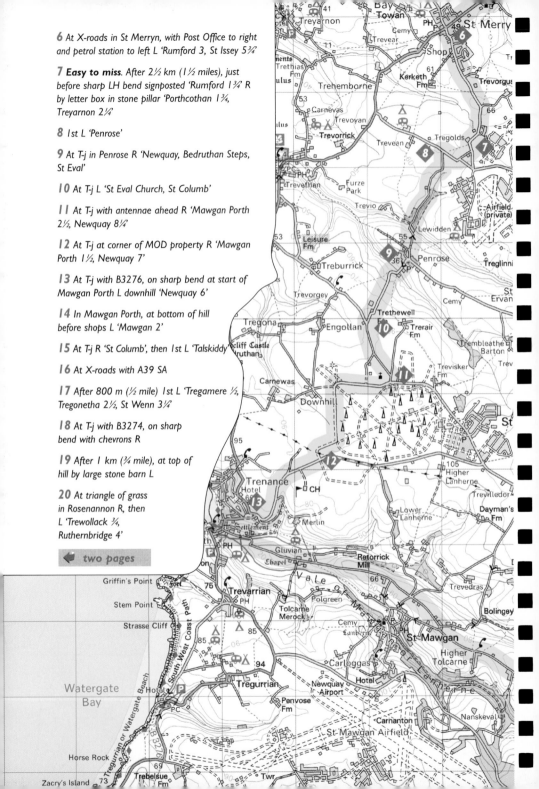

6 At X-roads in St Merryn, with Post Office to right and petrol station to left L 'Rumford 3, St Issey 5¾'

7 *Easy to miss*. After 2½ km (1½ miles), just before sharp LH bend signposted 'Rumford 1¾ R by letter box in stone pillar 'Porthcothan 1¾, Treyarnon 2¼'

8 1st L 'Penrose'

9 At T-j in Penrose R 'Newquay, Bedruthan Steps, St Eval'

10 At T-j L 'St Eval Church, St Columb'

11 At T-j with antennae ahead R 'Mawgan Porth 2½, Newquay 8¼'

12 At T-j at corner of MOD property R 'Mawgan Porth 1½, Newquay 7'

13 At T-j with B3276, on sharp bend at start of Mawgan Porth L downhill 'Newquay 6'

14 In Mawgan Porth, at bottom of hill before shops L 'Mawgan 2'

15 At T-j R 'St Columb', then 1st L 'Talskiddy'

16 At X-roads with A39 SA

17 After 800 m (½ mile) 1st L 'Tregamere ½, Tregonetha 2½, St Wenn 3¼'

18 At T-j with B3274, on sharp bend with chevrons R

19 After 1 km (¾ mile), at top of hill by large stone barn L

20 At triangle of grass in Rosenannon R, then L 'Trewollack ¾, Ruthernbridge 4'

◀ two pages

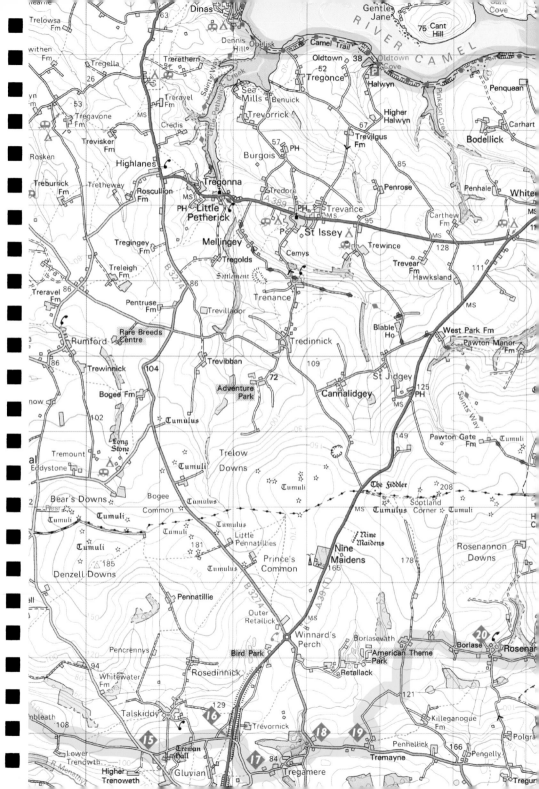

Along the edge of Bodmin Moor west of Launceston

7

This ride visits the attractive and little-known countryside lying north of Bodmin Moor. The views from Launceston Castle are most impressive, perhaps best appreciated after the ride, so that you can see where you have been. Starting from Launceston, a fast descent is followed by the steepest, although not the longest, climb of the route, from the valley of the River Kensey up to the church of St Stephens. You soon dive into the network of tiny lanes that criss-cross this part of Cornwall and pass through North Petherwin to Canworthy Water. You cross the River Ottery at Trengune and face a 176 m (580 ft) climb over 10 km (6 miles) to the edge of Bodmin. A long, gentle descent with lovely views (and the option of a detour to the pretty village of Altarnun) drops you down to cross the River Inny, another tributary of the Tamar. You then follow yet another river, the River Kensey, back to Launceston.

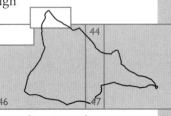

Start

The White Hart Hotel in the Square, Launceston

P Long-stay car park on the road towards Callington and Tavistock

Distance and grade

51 km (32 miles)
Moderate

Terrain

Two main climbs: 109 m (360 ft) at the start, just north of Launceston and a gentle 176m (580 ft) climb south from the River Ottery at Trengune to the edge of Bodmin Moor

Nearest railway

Liskeard, 24 km (15 miles) south of Launcestone

Launceston Langore North Petherwin Canworthy Water Trengune Trelash

Places of interest

Launceston 1

Launceston was the county capital until 1838. There has been settlement here for many years because of the advantages offered by its elevated position. The castle ruins show it to have been a Norman stronghold, though it was stormed four times during the Civil War. This castle, erstwhile seat of William the Conqueror's brother, still has its huge, round keep and from its walls, large areas of Cornwall and Devon can be seen. Ancient, narrow streets surround the town's main square and among the many interesting Georgian buildings is Lawrence House in Castle Street, now a museum of local history. Lavish carvings cover the Church of St Mary Magdalene.

Refreshments

Lots of choice in Launceston
Old Wainhouse PH,
Wainhouse Corner
Wilsey Down PH, Hallworthy
Rising Sun PH, near Altarnun

Tamar Otter Park *(near North Petherwin)* 6

Otters are bred here in natural surroundings. There are also waterfowl, deer and a nature trail.

Altarnun *(1½ km (1 mile) off the route)* 16

Cottages of slate and granite line Altarnun's single, winding street. By the entrance to the churchyard, a medieval packhorse bridge crosses the peat-stained stream known as Penpont Water. The old moorstone church is dedicated to St Nonna, mother of St David of Wales. Just inside the churchyard is a Celtic cross said to date from the 6th century. The 79 carved bench ends depict travelling musicians and entertainers, local characters of the time and a flock of sheep.

Hallworthy   Higher Basil   Tregunnon   Trewen   Pipers Pool

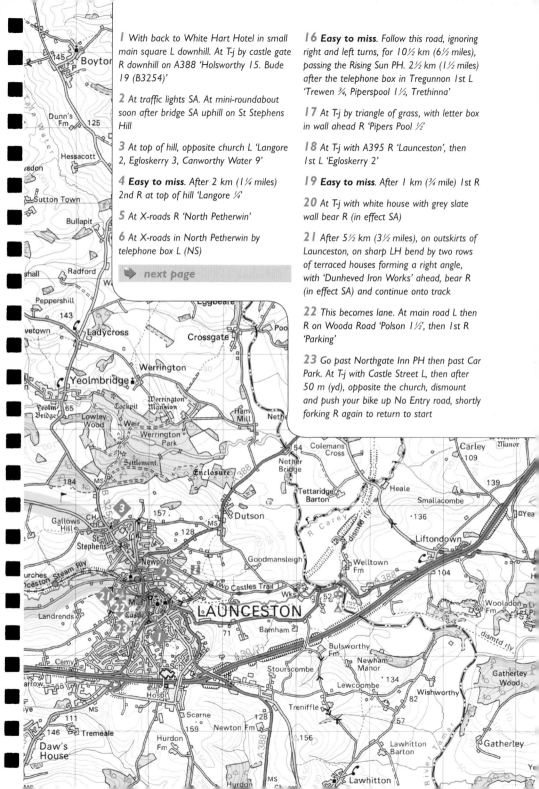

1 With back to White Hart Hotel in small main square L downhill. At T-j by castle gate R downhill on A388 'Holsworthy 15. Bude 19 (B3254)'

2 At traffic lights SA. At mini-roundabout soon after bridge SA uphill on St Stephens Hill

3 At top of hill, opposite church L 'Langore 2, Egloskerry 3, Canworthy Water 9'

4 Easy to miss. After 2 km (1¼ miles) 2nd R at top of hill 'Langore ¼'

5 At X-roads R 'North Petherwin'

6 At X-roads in North Petherwin by telephone box L (NS)

next page

16 Easy to miss. Follow this road, ignoring right and left turns, for 10½ km (6½ miles), passing the Rising Sun PH. 2½ km (1½ miles) after the telephone box in Tregunnon 1st L 'Trewen ¾, Piperspool 1½, Trethinna'

17 At T-j by triangle of grass, with letter box in wall ahead R 'Pipers Pool ½'

18 At T-j with A395 R 'Launceston', then 1st L 'Egloskerry 2'

19 Easy to miss. After 1 km (¾ mile) 1st R

20 At T-j with white house with grey slate wall bear R (in effect SA)

21 After 5½ km (3½ miles), on outskirts of Launceston, on sharp LH bend by two rows of terraced houses forming a right angle, with 'Dunheved Iron Works' ahead, bear R (in effect SA) and continue onto track

22 This becomes lane. At main road L then R on Wooda Road 'Polson 1½', then 1st R 'Parking'

23 Go past Northgate Inn PH then past Car Park. At T-j with Castle Street L, then after 50 m (yd), opposite the church, dismount and push your bike up No Entry road, shortly forking R again to return to start

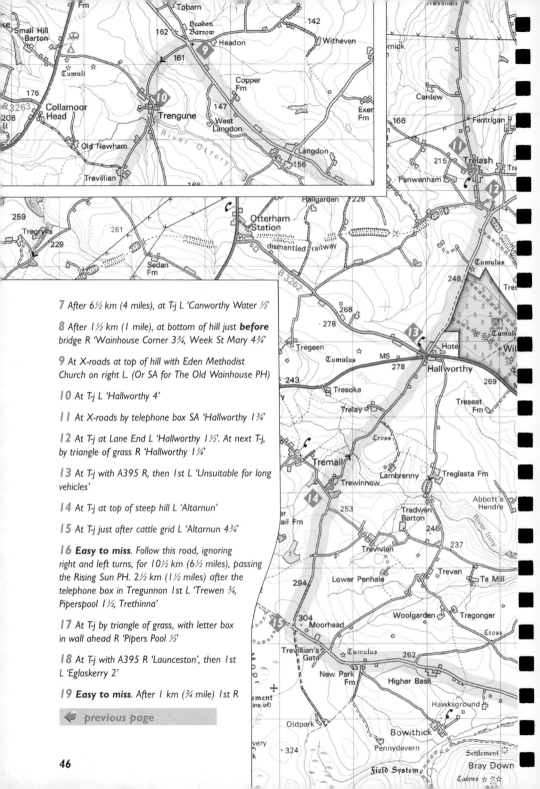

7 After 6½ km (4 miles), at T-j L 'Canworthy Water ½'

8 After 1½ km (1 mile), at bottom of hill just **before** bridge R 'Wainhouse Corner 3¾, Week St Mary 4¾'

9 At X-roads at top of hill with Eden Methodist Church on right L. (Or SA for The Old Wainhouse PH)

10 At T-j L 'Hallworthy 4'

11 At X-roads by telephone box SA 'Hallworthy 1¾'

12 At T-j at Lane End L 'Hallworthy 1½'. At next T-j, by triangle of grass R 'Hallworthy 1¼'

13 At T-j with A395 R, then 1st L 'Unsuitable for long vehicles'

14 At T-j at top of steep hill L 'Altarnun'

15 At T-j just after cattle grid L 'Altarnun 4¾'

16 Easy to miss. Follow this road, ignoring right and left turns, for 10½ km (6½ miles), passing the Rising Sun PH. 2½ km (1½ miles) after the telephone box in Tregunnon 1st L 'Trewen ¾, Piperspool 1½, Trethinna'

17 At T-j by triangle of grass, with letter box in wall ahead R 'Pipers Pool ½'

18 At T-j with A395 R 'Launceston', then 1st L 'Egloskerry 2'

19 Easy to miss. After 1 km (¾ mile) 1st R

⬅ previous page

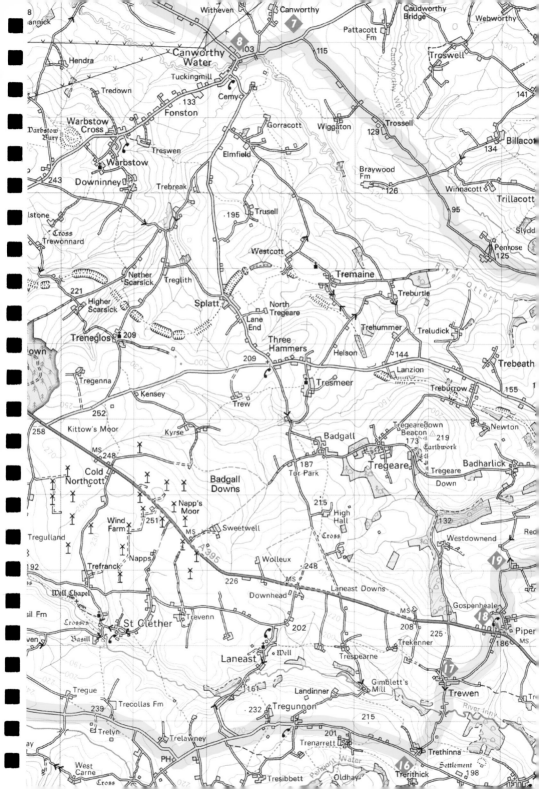

8 In and out of the Tamar valley between Tavistock and Launceston

The River Tamar, and the deep valley it has cut, forms a natural boundary between Devon and Cornwall from the south coast at Plymouth to its source northeast of Bude. This ride explores the little-visited area between Tavistock and Launceston. It crosses the river via two of the smaller and quieter bridges at Horsebridge and Greystone Bridge, both crossings involving steep descents into and steep climbs out of the valley. Starting at Tavistock, the ride heads west on quiet lanes, passing the Chipshop Inn with its enticing placard. The lanes get even smaller as you descend to the Tamar and the excellent pub at Horsebridge. From here to Launceston, the route runs across the grain of the land and crosses four valleys in quick succession. The castle in Launceston is well worth a visit. After Launceston, a steep descent into the Tamar valley is followed by the longest climb of the ride, rewarded with wide-ranging views towards Dartmoor. The ride ends with a satisfying 6½ km (4 mile) descent.

52   53

50   51

Start

The Town Hall, Tavistock

P Long-stay car park on the A390 Plymouth Road

Distance and grade

46 km (29 miles)

///// Strenuous

Terrain

Two major climbs: one of 131 m (430 ft) northwest from Horsebridge and one of 228 m (750 ft) east from Greystone Bridge. Several hills of between 45 and 76 m (150 and 250 ft), including four in a row north from the River Inny to Launceston

Nearest railway

Plymouth, 24 km (15 miles) south of Tavistock

Tavistock   Millhill   Horsebridge   Pempwell   Bealsmill   Treburley   Trekenner   Lezant

Tavistock 1

The town began in the prehistoric camp that can still be traced on the hill beside Kelly College. Much later, the Saxons built an abbey that the Danes burnt down; it was rebuilt, however, and became the largest and most important religious house in the Southwest. Its wealth, like that of the town, was based upon wool, cloth and then tin. In 1281, Tavistock was designated a stannary town – an official centre for assaying and stamping tin. The discovery of copper, in the late 18th century, led to a huge mining boom; the Devon Great Consols was the richest copper mine in Europe. Copper ore was transported down to the Tamar by a 6½ km (4 mile) canal, part of which still runs through the park. The town was granted to the Russell family, the Dukes of Bedford, and they owned it until 1911. During the 19th century, they virtually rebuilt the castellated town centre around Bedford Square. Sir Francis Drake was born in Tavistock.

Refreshments

Lots of choice in Tavistock
Chipshop Inn PH, Chipshop *The
Royal PH* 🍴🍴, Horsebridge
Springer Spaniel PH, Treburley
Lots of choice in Launceston

Launceston 16

Launceston is set on a hillside and crowned by the ruins of a 13th-century castle. Built on the site of an earlier wooden fortification, this fortress once guarded the main route from Cornwall to Devon. It was later used as an assize court and a prison and until 1821, public hangings were held on the castle green. A wall was built around Launceston in the reign of Henry III. The granite-stone church of St Mary Magdalene is covered in carvings.

Launceston   Leburnick   Greystone Bridge   Ramsdown Cross   Longcross   Hurdwick Farm

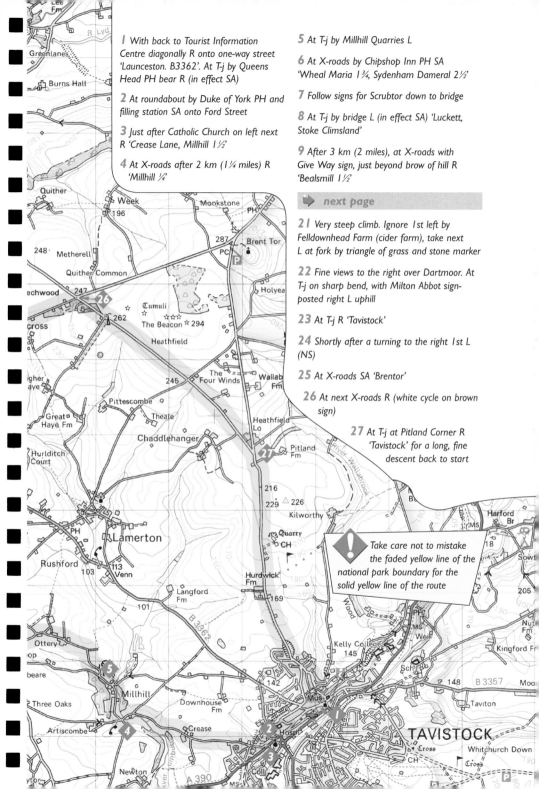

1 With back to Tourist Information Centre diagonally R onto one-way street 'Launceston. B3362'. At T-j by Queens Head PH bear R (in effect SA)

2 At roundabout by Duke of York PH and filling station SA onto Ford Street

3 Just after Catholic Church on left next R 'Crease Lane, Millhill 1½'

4 At X-roads after 2 km (1¼ miles) R 'Millhill ¼'

5 At T-j by Millhill Quarries L

6 At X-roads by Chipshop Inn PH SA 'Wheal Maria 1¾, Sydenham Dameral 2½'

7 Follow signs for Scrubtor down to bridge

8 At T-j by bridge L (in effect SA) 'Luckett, Stoke Climsland'

9 After 3 km (2 miles), at X-roads with Give Way sign, just beyond brow of hill R 'Bealsmill 1½'

next page

21 Very steep climb. Ignore 1st left by Felldownhead Farm (cider farm), take next L at fork by triangle of grass and stone marker

22 Fine views to the right over Dartmoor. At T-j on sharp bend, with Milton Abbot sign-posted right L uphill

23 At T-j R 'Tavistock'

24 Shortly after a turning to the right 1st L (NS)

25 At X-roads SA 'Brentor'

26 At next X-roads R (white cycle on brown sign)

27 At T-j at Pitland Corner R 'Tavistock' for a long, fine descent back to start

> ⚠ Take care not to mistake the faded yellow line of the national park boundary for the solid yellow line of the route

9 After 3 km (2 miles), at X-roads with Give Way sign, just beyond brow of hill R 'Bealsmill 1½'

10 Over bridge and steeply up. At X-roads with A388 by Springer Spaniel PH SA 'Trekenner ½, Trebullett 1½'

11 Shortly fork R 'Trekenner ¼, Lezant 1'

12 At offset X-roads in Lezant L, then R past telephone box

13 At T-j after steep hill L (NS)

14 At next T-j, by barn with corrugated-iron roof R 'South Petherwin 2½'

15 At off-set X-roads SA

16 At X-roads shortly after crossing A30 R on Tavistock Road 'A388 Callington 10½, A384 Tavistock 13½ (or L here for Launceston town centre, return to this point to continue route)

17 On sharp RH bend with chevrons L 'Stourscombe, Lawhitton 1½'

18 At X-roads with B3362 SA 'Leburnick'

19 Steeply down to river, ignoring lefts and rights. At T-j with traffic lights R over Greystone Bridge

20 Ignore L immediately by river, take next L after 100 m (yd) 'Bradstone Kelly, Lifton'

21 Very steep climb. Ignore 1st left by Felldownhead Farm (cider farm), take next L at fork by triangle of grass and stone marker

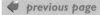

previous page

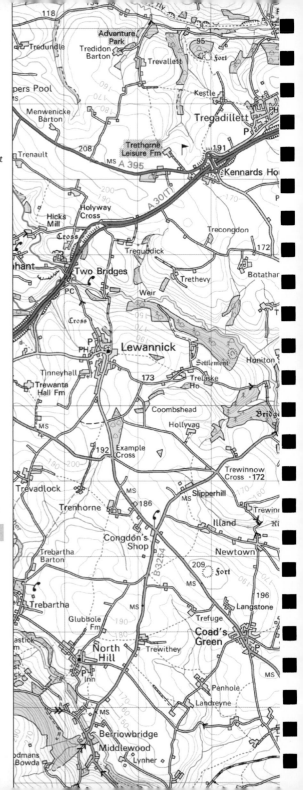

9 South from Kingsbridge across the South Hams to Prawle Point

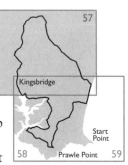

This is a tough but rewarding ride, with over 760 m (2500 ft) of climbing and some magnificent views of the South Hams and out to sea. A steep climb out of Kingsbridge is soon followed by a swift descent into the valley of the River Avon. The ride climbs out of the valley onto the ridge above Moreleigh. The next 8 km (5 miles) should be savoured as this is the only flattish section on quiet lanes in the whole ride. Views of the sea open up and you soon drop into the pretty village of Slapton and past the unusual freshwater lake of Slapton Ley. The best sea views are from East Prawle, although you will need to lose some height and divert off the main route for a clear view of the coastline. Dropping down towards East Portlemouth, you have some splendid views of Salcombe and up the Kingsbridge Estuary. Either side of South Pool, you are faced with some of the steepest hills in the whole ride. Once you have reached Frogmore, however, fairly flat 5 km (3 miles) along the A379 take you back to the start.

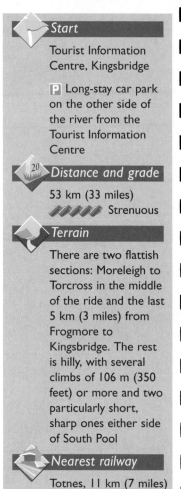

Start

Tourist Information Centre, Kingsbridge

P Long-stay car park on the other side of the river from the Tourist Information Centre

Distance and grade

53 km (33 miles)

Strenuous

Terrain

There are two flattish sections: Moreleigh to Torcross in the middle of the ride and the last 5 km (3 miles) from Frogmore to Kingsbridge. The rest is hilly, with several climbs of 106 m (350 feet) or more and two particularly short, sharp ones either side of South Pool

Nearest railway

Totnes, 11 km (7 miles) north of Moreleigh

Kingsbridge

Woodleigh

Hendham

Moreleigh

Wallaton Cross

Lower Green Cross

Slapton

Kingsbridge 1

Kingsbridge is an old town with Georgian houses and an Elizabethan arcade. The Victorian building with an onion- shaped clocktower serves as town hall, theatre and market. The Cookworthy Museum in Fore Street houses a display of rural life.

Slapton Ley 9

Wildfowl and rare marsh birds find sanctuary in this 270-acre freshwater lake, which is cut off from the sea by Slapton Sands. An obelisk commemorates US soldiers who used the sands to rehearse the Normandy landings.

Slapton Ley from above Torcross

Torcross 11

Pleasant old houses line the seafront along Start Bay at Torcross.

Prawle Point 13

This is the southernmost tip of Devon. The name 'Prawle' is derived from the Old English for 'lookout' and there are magnificent views.

Kingsbridge Estuary 16-18

The estuary is so sheltered that plants bloom and fruit ripens early; there is a profusion of palms, cypresses and wild flowers.

Refreshments

Lots of choice in Kingsbridge
New Inn PH 🍷, Moreleigh
Tower Inn PH 🍷🍷, *Queens Arms PH* 🍷, Slapton
Start Bay PH 🍷🍷 *and others in* Torcross
Providence Inn, Pigs Nose Inn PH 🍷, *Piglet Stores and Café,* East Prawle
Millbrook Inn PH 🍷🍷, South Pool

Cousin's Cross East Prawle East Portemouth South Pool Frogmore West Charleton

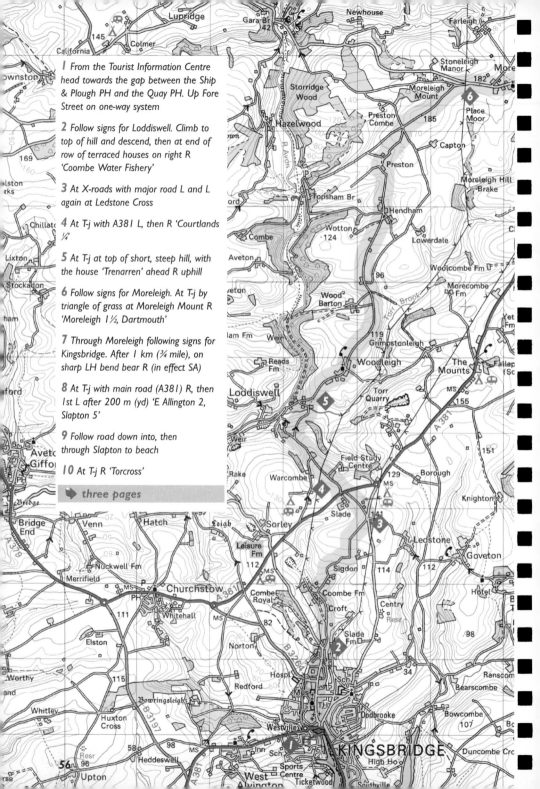

1 From the Tourist Information Centre head towards the gap between the Ship & Plough PH and the Quay PH. Up Fore Street on one-way system

2 Follow signs for Loddiswell. Climb to top of hill and descend, then at end of row of terraced houses on right R 'Coombe Water Fishery'

3 At X-roads with major road L and L again at Ledstone Cross

4 At T-j with A381 L, then R 'Courtlands ¼'

5 At T-j at top of short, steep hill, with the house 'Trenarren' ahead R uphill

6 Follow signs for Moreleigh. At T-j by triangle of grass at Moreleigh Mount R 'Moreleigh 1½, Dartmouth'

7 Through Moreleigh following signs for Kingsbridge. After 1 km (¾ mile), on sharp LH bend bear R (in effect SA)

8 At T-j with main road (A381) R, then 1st L after 200 m (yd) 'E Allington 2, Slapton 5'

9 Follow road down into, then through Slapton to beach

10 At T-j R 'Torcross'

➡ **three pages**

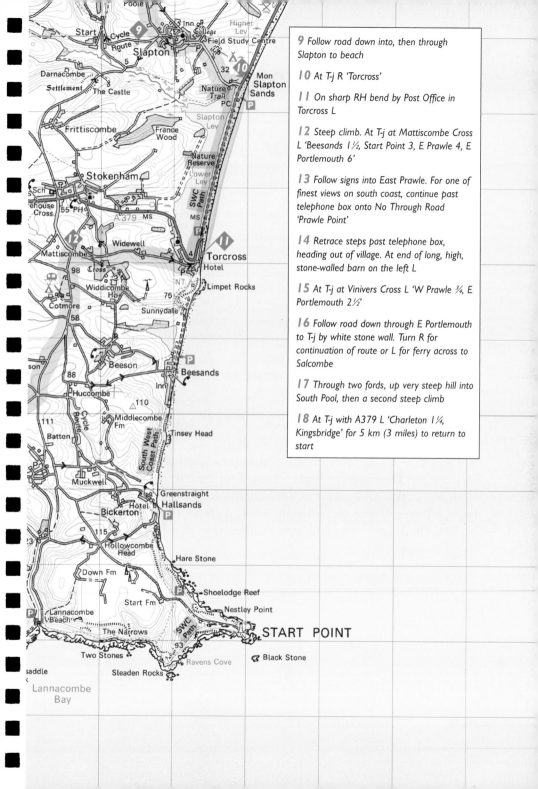

9 Follow road down into, then through Slapton to beach

10 At T-j R 'Torcross'

11 On sharp RH bend by Post Office in Torcross L

12 Steep climb. At T-j at Mattiscombe Cross L 'Beesands 1½, Start Point 3, E Prawle 4, E Portlemouth 6'

13 Follow signs into East Prawle. For one of finest views on south coast, continue past telephone box onto No Through Road 'Prawle Point'

14 Retrace steps past telephone box, heading out of village. At end of long, high, stone-walled barn on the left L

15 At T-j at Vinivers Cross L 'W Prawle ¾, E Portlemouth 2½'

16 Follow road down through E Portlemouth to T-j by white stone wall. Turn R for continuation of route or L for ferry across to Salcombe

17 Through two fords, up very steep hill into South Pool, then a second steep climb

18 At T-j with A379 L 'Charleton 1¼, Kingsbridge' for 5 km (3 miles) to return to start

From Moretonhampstead onto the eastern edge of Dartmoor

Start

The Bell Inn PH, Moretonhampstead

P Long-stay car park on road towards Princetown

Distance and grade

46 km (29 miles)

///// Strenuous

Terrain

Three main climbs: 134 m (440 ft) south from Chagford, 122 m (400 ft) south from Widecombe (very steep) and 152 m (500 ft) northwest from Lustleigh

Nearest railway

Crediton, 18 km (11 miles) northeast of Moretonhampstead

This is a tough ride with some steep hills to climb, notably out of Chagford, Widecombe and Lustleigh. The scenery is magnificent, the villages full of interest and there are some fine pubs and tea stops on the way. The route leaves Moretonhampstead on a delightful lane with lovely views across to the moor. Chagford has a lively atmosphere and makes a good early stopping point. A stiff climb takes you onto the moor. The views west towards Hamel Down are magnificent and you are soon on a tiny road to Widecombe. You will probably share the delights of Widecombe with the odd coachload, but it is somewhat unlikely that they will follow you up the northwest face of Pudsham Down! The views from the top are ample reward. An excellent descent to Owlacombe Cross leaves you at the start of a labyrinth of lanes that will take you through Bovey Tracey to Lustleigh. Enjoy a choice of refreshments before the final challenge – the climb up onto the ridge that leads to Moretonhampstead.

Moretonhampstead

Easton

Chagford

Beetor Cross

Widecombe in the Moor

Cold East Cr

Moretonhampstead 1

This small town on the northeastern edge of Dartmoor is 213 m (700 ft) above sea level. The granite Almshouses date from 1637 and have a colonnade and thatched roof.

Widecombe 9

Widecombe is the best known and the most commercialized of the Dartmoor villages. It stands at 244 m (800 ft) and is dominated by the 36 m (120 ft) tower of its fine 14th-century church. An elaborately carved sign depicting Old Uncle Tom Cobleigh commemorates 'Widdicome Fair', the song that made the village famous. A fair is still held on the second Tuesday in September.

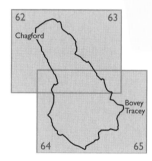

Refreshments

White Hart PH 🍽️🍽️ *and others in* Moretonhampstead *Bullers Inn PH* 🍽️ *and others in* Chagford *Olde Inn PH* 🍽️, *Rugglestone PH* 🍽️ *and others in* Widecombe *Edgemoor PH* 🍽️ *and others in* Bovey Tracey *Cleeve Hotel PH* 🍽️🍽️, *tea shop,* Lustleigh

Owlacombe Cross   Sigford   Willis's Cross   Bovey Tracey   Lustleigh

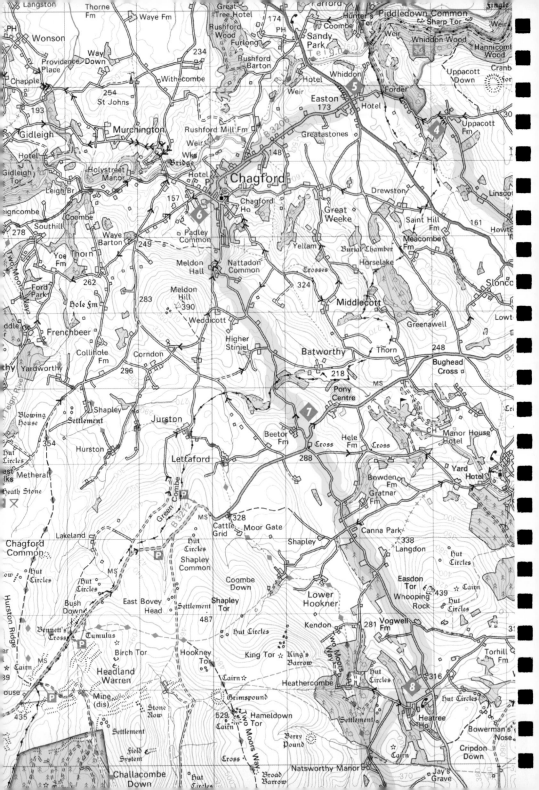

1 With back to the Bell Inn PH R on A382 'Okehampton'

2 300 m (yd) after passing hospital on the right next R at Chagford Cross 'Howton'. After 50 m (yd) 1st L 'Howton'

3 At T-j by triangle of grass at Howton Cross L 'Howton'. At fork after 100 m (yd) by 'Tom Cobbley's Springwater' R

4 Lovely views on left. At T-j by rose trellis L 'Chagford'

5 At X-roads with A382 SA onto B3206 'Chagford 1½'

6 At T-j in Chagford L 'Health Centre, Postbridge 7'

7 Follow signs for Postbridge. At T-j with B3212 at Beetor Cross R, then 1st L 'Manaton 1'

8 This section can be surprisingly busy. At X-roads at Heatree Cross R 'Heathercombe, Natsworthy'

➡ two pages

21 Just over bridge 1st L 'Lustleigh'

22 At T-j on sharp bend bear R (in effect SA) 'Lustleigh, Moreton' (sign is hidden on the right)

23 At T-j on sharp bend, with row of terraced houses to the right L downhill 'Lustleigh'

24 Follow through into Lustleigh to see the village and stop for refreshments. Do a circuit of the church, turning R at Post Office, L at next T-j, then 1st L uphill 'Unsuitable for lorries'

25 **Easy to miss**. Steep, then gentle climb. After 5½ km (3½ miles), shortly after passing a signpost for Manaton to the left and Narramore Farm to the right next R at Brinning Cross (NS)

26 At T-j R to return to Moretonhampstead. At T-j in Moretonhampstead R to return to start

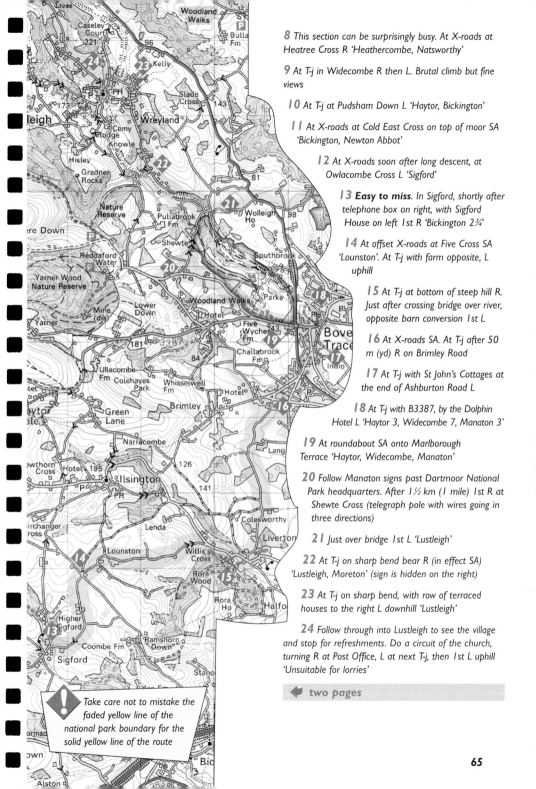

8 This section can be surprisingly busy. At X-roads at Heatree Cross R 'Heathercombe, Natsworthy'

9 At T-j in Widecombe R then L. Brutal climb but fine views

10 At T-j at Pudsham Down L 'Haytor, Bickington'

11 At X-roads at Cold East Cross on top of moor SA 'Bickington, Newton Abbot'

12 At X-roads soon after long descent, at Owlacombe Cross L 'Sigford'

13 **Easy to miss**. In Sigford, shortly after telephone box on right, with Sigford House on left 1st R 'Bickington 2¾'

14 At offset X-roads at Five Cross SA 'Lounston'. At T-j with farm opposite, L uphill

15 At T-j at bottom of steep hill R. Just after crossing bridge over river, opposite barn conversion 1st L

16 At X-roads SA. At T-j after 50 m (yd) R on Brimley Road

17 At T-j with St John's Cottages at the end of Ashburton Road L

18 At T-j with B3387, by the Dolphin Hotel L 'Haytor 3, Widecombe 7, Manaton 3'

19 At roundabout SA onto Marlborough Terrace 'Haytor, Widecombe, Manaton'

20 Follow Manaton signs past Dartmoor National Park headquarters. After 1½ km (1 mile) 1st R at Shewte Cross (telegraph pole with wires going in three directions)

21 Just over bridge 1st L 'Lustleigh'

22 At T-j on sharp bend bear R (in effect SA) 'Lustleigh, Moreton' (sign is hidden on the right)

23 At T-j on sharp bend, with row of terraced houses to the right L downhill 'Lustleigh'

24 Follow through into Lustleigh to see the village and stop for refreshments. Do a circuit of the church, turning R at Post Office, L at next T-j, then 1st L uphill 'Unsuitable for lorries'

◀ **two pages**

Take care not to mistake the faded yellow line of the national park boundary for the solid yellow line of the route

Rolling hills north from Holsworthy to Bradworthy

Start

The church in Holsworthy

P Near the church, follow signs

Devon has many 'forgotten' corners, perhaps none more so than this area in the far west of the county. It has an unspoilt and unchanging atmosphere, far from 20th-century bustle and far from tourists towing caravans and crawling from one hyped tourist honeypot to the next. The area is predominantly agricultural with hamlets of farms and cottages interspersed among larger villages such as Bradworthy and Shebbear.

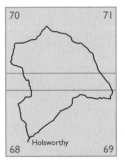

Distance and grade

48 km (30 miles)
Moderate

Terrain

Rolling more than hilly. Most of the ride lies between 36 and 57 m (120 and 190 ft) with no climbs of more than 60 m (200 ft)

Nearest railway

Barnstaple, 29 km (18 miles) east of Stibb Cross

The ride heads north on quiet lanes, dipping to cross a tributary of the River Torridge south of Bradworthy, and then crossing the river itself near West Putford. A 13 km (8 mile) ridge-ride from Powler's Piece through Stibb Cross to Shebbear takes you across what is almost moorland. Tiny lanes lead west from Shebbear past the lovely thatched house in Thornbury and through Woodacott Cross back to Holsworthy.

Refreshments

Lots of choice in Holsworthy
Bradworthy Inn PH, Pigs Ear PH 🍺, Bradworthy
Tea shop, Powler's Piece
Union Inn PH, Stibb Cross
Devil's Stone Inn PH, Shebbear

Holsworthy · Thuborough Barton · Sutcombe · Bradworthy · Kismeldon Bridge · Powler's Piece

Holsworthy 1

Situated on a high ridge between the lovely valleys of the Rivers Tamar and Torridge, Holsworthy springs to life on Wednesdays with a fine old-fashioned market selling local

cheese and butter, Devonshire cream and good poultry. In the church is a beautifully carved, 17th-century organ, sold from Chelsea Old Church to Bideford in 1723 as 'worn out'. The town has a dubious claim to fame as it was the last place in England where a man was punished by being put in the stocks. During the first half of the 20th-century, it was an important railway halt and a busy livestock centre. The railway was closed in the 1960s but the impressive viaducts can be walked with permission from British Rail.

West Putford 12

In a woodland garden is an unbelievable collection of over 1000 gnomes and pixies; you can watch the pottery pixies being made.

Thornbury 17

The Devon Museum of Mechanical

Holsworthy High Street

Music houses a fascinating collection of working musical instruments.

Blagdonmoor Wharf 18/19

The wharf at Blagdon used to be the terminal of the now-defunct Bude-Holsworthy Canal.

Thorne Moor Stibb Cross Shebbear Gidcott Mill Thornbury Woodacott Cross

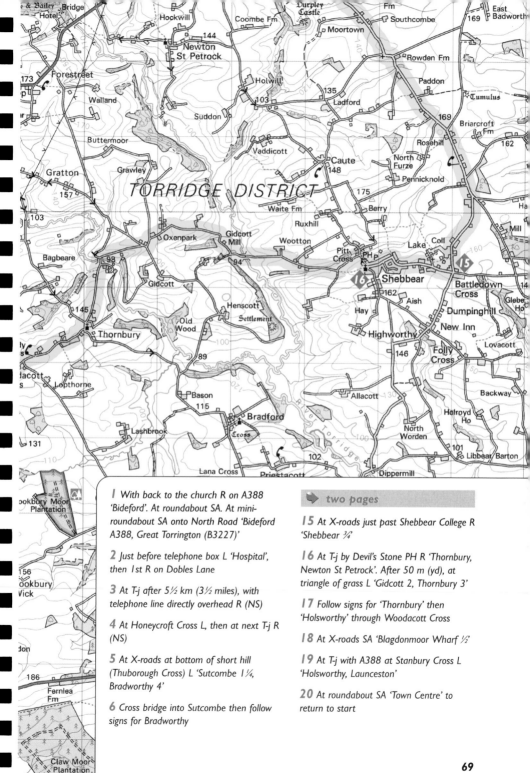

1 With back to the church R on A388 'Bideford'. At roundabout SA. At mini-roundabout SA onto North Road 'Bideford A388, Great Torrington (B3227)'

2 Just before telephone box L 'Hospital', then 1st R on Dobles Lane

3 At T-j after 5½ km (3½ miles), with telephone line directly overhead R (NS)

4 At Honeycroft Cross L, then at next T-j R (NS)

5 At X-roads at bottom of short hill (Thuborough Cross) L 'Sutcombe 1¼, Bradworthy 4'

6 Cross bridge into Sutcombe then follow signs for Bradworthy

two pages

15 At X-roads just past Shebbear College R 'Shebbear ¾'

16 At T-j by Devil's Stone PH R 'Thornbury, Newton St Petrock'. After 50 m (yd), at triangle of grass L 'Gidcott 2, Thornbury 3'

17 Follow signs for 'Thornbury' then 'Holsworthy' through Woodacott Cross

18 At X-roads SA 'Blagdonmoor Wharf ½'

19 At T-j with A388 at Stanbury Cross L 'Holsworthy, Launceston'

20 At roundabout SA 'Town Centre' to return to start

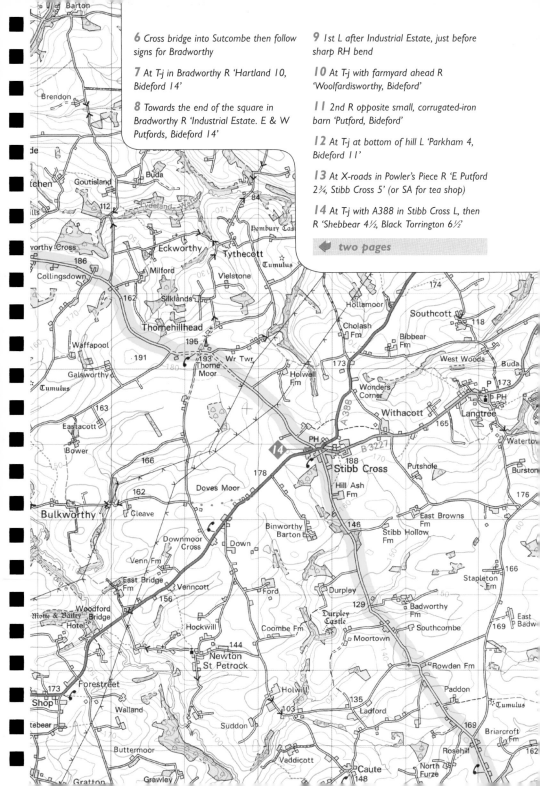

6 Cross bridge into Sutcombe then follow signs for Bradworthy

7 At T-j in Bradworthy R 'Hartland 10, Bideford 14'

8 Towards the end of the square in Bradworthy R 'Industrial Estate. E & W Putfords, Bideford 14'

9 1st L after Industrial Estate, just before sharp RH bend

10 At T-j with farmyard ahead R 'Woolfardisworthy, Bideford'

11 2nd R opposite small, corrugated-iron barn 'Putford, Bideford'

12 At T-j at bottom of hill L 'Parkham 4, Bideford 11'

13 At X-roads in Powler's Piece R 'E Putford 2¾, Stibb Cross 5' (or SA for tea shop)

14 At T-j with A388 in Stibb Cross L, then R 'Shebbear 4½, Black Torrington 6½'

two pages

12 *Rolling Devon hills west from Crediton to Morchard Bishop and North Tawton*

Start

The Ship PH, Crediton High Street

P Follow signs for long-stay car park

Distance and grade

48 km (30 miles)

Moderate/strenuous

Terrain

Many short hills and three longer ones: 106 m (350 ft) to Newbuildings, 91 m (300 ft) after crossing River Yeo near Lapford and 100 m (330 ft) up to Spreyton

Nearest railway

Crediton

Lying in the heart of Devon, between Dartmoor and Exmoor, this area is little-visited by tourists. It is, nevertheless, an area of great charm and is completely unspoilt. The ride links Crediton, with its vast, red-sandstone church, to Morchard Bishop and North Tawton via two fine ridges. There are wonderful views of the soft folds of Devon's hills, particularly from the second ridge. Morchard Bishop is famous for its row of terraced, thatched houses. Both Morchard Bishop and North Tawton serve as focal points for the hamlets lying nearby. You pass through Spreyton, where Tom Cobley is buried, and then into lovely woodland either side of the valley formed by the River Troney. The last climb back into Crediton is the least welcome part of the ride.

Refreshments

Ship PH and others in Crediton
London Inn PH, Morchard Bishop
Copper Key PH and others in North Tawton
Tom Cobbley Tavern PH, Spreyton

Crediton

Newbuildings

Oldborough

Morchard Bishop

Kelland Cross

Leigh Cross

Crediton 1

Devon's Cathedral City has been a Christian centre since Saxon times. It is reputed to be the birthplace of Winfrith (AD 608), who later became St Boniface. The massive, red-sandstone Church of the Holy Cross is mainly 15th-century,

In Spreyton Wood

although parts date back to 1150. The Chapter House has Cromwellian relics, including a well-preserved buckskin coat and boots.

North Tawton 11

The riverside settlement of North Tawton dates back to Roman times, when the fort of Nemetostatio, strategically located on the route to Cornwall, was based here. In 1374, it was granted its first market charter and remained an important trading centre until the beginning of this century. The church dates from the 15th century and has a spire tiled with oak shingles.

Spreyton 15

An attractive small village, Spreyton has connections with 'Uncle Tom Cobley' of Widecome Fair song fame: he was born nearby and is buried in Spreyton churchyard. The 15th-century church tower was kept whitewashed in former days as a guide for mariners. As Spreyton is the highest hamlet in Devon, both coastlines can be seen from the church tower on a fine day.

North Tawton

Itton

Heath Cross
Spreyton

Road Down Cross

Yeoford

Moorlake

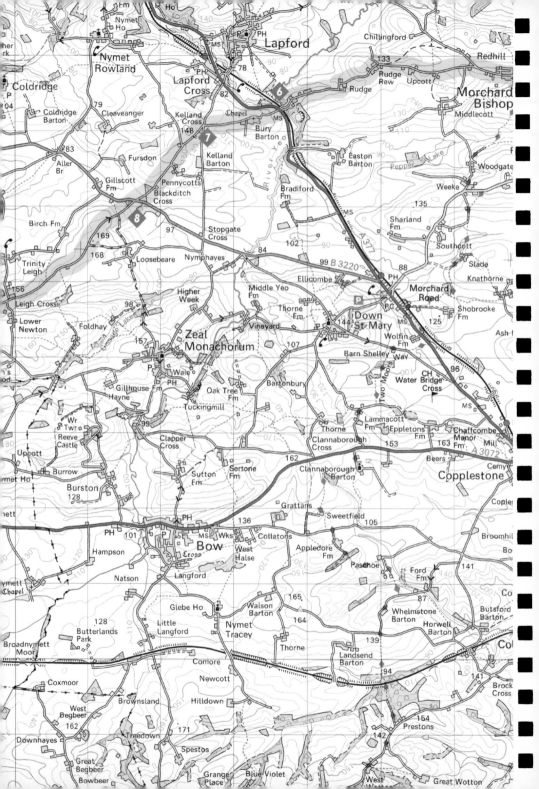

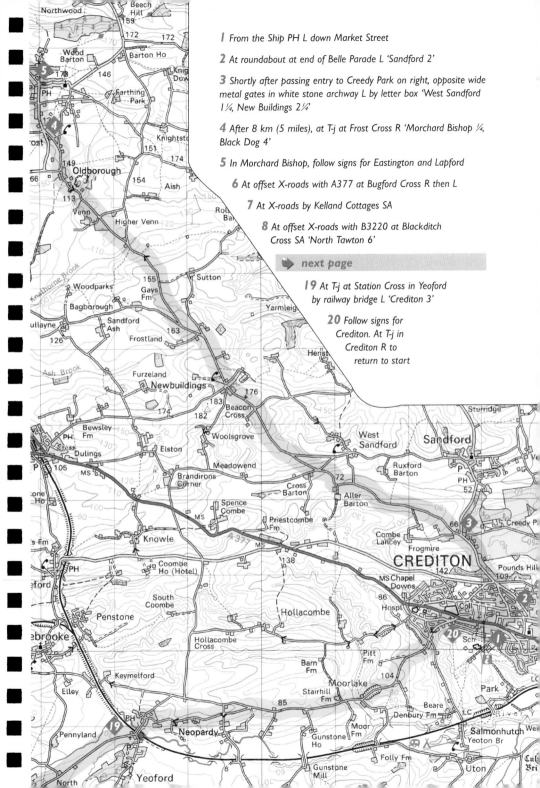

1 From the Ship PH L down Market Street

2 At roundabout at end of Belle Parade L 'Sandford 2'

3 Shortly after passing entry to Creedy Park on right, opposite wide metal gates in white stone archway L by letter box 'West Sandford 1¼, New Buildings 2¼'

4 After 8 km (5 miles), at T-j at Frost Cross R 'Morchard Bishop ¼, Black Dog 4'

5 In Morchard Bishop, follow signs for Eastington and Lapford

6 At offset X-roads with A377 at Bugford Cross R then L

7 At X-roads by Kelland Cottages SA

8 At offset X-roads with B3220 at Blackditch Cross SA 'North Tawton 6'

➡ next page

19 At T-j at Station Cross in Yeoford by railway bridge L 'Crediton 3'

20 Follow signs for Crediton. At T-j in Crediton R to return to start

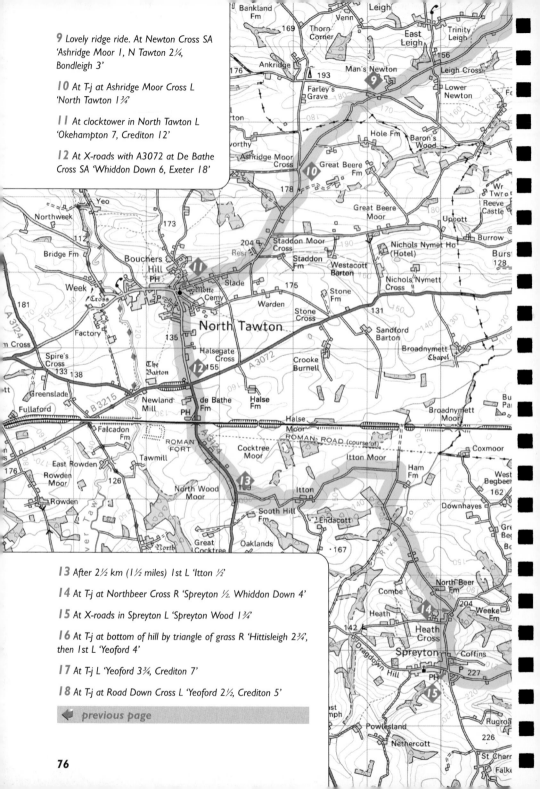

9 *Lovely ridge ride. At Newton Cross SA 'Ashridge Moor 1, N Tawton 2¼, Bondleigh 3'*

10 *At T-j at Ashridge Moor Cross L 'North Tawton 1¾'*

11 *At clocktower in North Tawton L 'Okehampton 7, Crediton 12'*

12 *At X-roads with A3072 at De Bathe Cross SA 'Whiddon Down 6, Exeter 18'*

13 *After 2½ km (1½ miles) 1st L 'Itton ½'*

14 *At T-j at Northbeer Cross R 'Spreyton ½, Whiddon Down 4'*

15 *At X-roads in Spreyton L 'Spreyton Wood 1¾'*

16 *At T-j at bottom of hill by triangle of grass R 'Hittisleigh 2¾, then 1st L 'Yeoford 4'*

17 *At T-j L 'Yeoford 3¾, Crediton 7'*

18 *At T-j at Road Down Cross L 'Yeoford 2½, Crediton 5'*

◀ previous page

From South Molton to the roof of Exmoor

Start

The Clocktower, South Molton

P Long-stay car park south of the High Street

Distance and grade

48 km (30 miles)

Strenuous

Terrain

Two climbs: 183 m (600 feet) north from Yarnacott to Stone Cross and 366 m (1200 feet) from Brayford to Hangley Cleave on top of Exmoor

Nearest railway

Barnstaple, 8 km (5 miles) west of Yarnacott

This ride features a reasonably good ridge and descent. Needless to say, you have to earn these delights by climbing two long, tough hills. It is worth waiting for a clear day to do this ride as the views from along the ridge are truly stupendous. The ride starts from the unspoilt, unpretentious town of South Molton, the focal point for south west Exmoor. It then heads west, parallel with the busy North Devon link road, as far as Yarnacott. The first big hill, with a particularly savage start near Yarnacott, climbs 183 m (600 ft) to Kimbland Cross, above Brayford. Ahead of you, lies the next challenge – a descent into

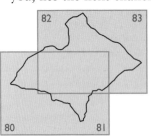

the valley to cross the River Bray at the village of Brayford and a 366 m (1200 ft) climb via Five Cross Way to Mole's Chamber. The next 16 km (10 miles), 10 km (6 miles) across the roof of Exmoor then 6 km (4 miles) down to North Molton, must rate amongst the very finest in the country; there's even a pub at the end of the ridge and before the downhill. An unexpected short climb needs to be tackled to pass through North Molton on the way back to the start.

South Molton　Shallowford　Riverton　Yarnacott　Stone Cross　Brayford　Five Cr... Way

South Molton 1

Between the Middle Ages and the mid-19th century, South Molton became a thriving wool town. It was also a coach stop on the route to Barnstaple and Bideford, and the nearest town to the iron and copper mines of North Molton. The many fine Georgian and Victorian houses, particularly the grand 18th-century Guildhall and 19th-century Assembly Rooms, were built with profits from wool and minerals. The 15th-century church has a medieval stone pulpit and handsome figure carvings in the nave.

Exmoor

Quince Honey Farm, South Molton 1

Wild Exmoor honeybees live here in their natural habitats. This is Britain's largest working honey farm and includes press-button hives that open to reveal the centre of the colony.

North Devon Farm Park, Swimbridge 7

Rare breeds of cattle, sheep, poultry and waterfowl roam the 25 acres of this park.

Refreshments

Old Coaching Inn PH 🍺 *and others in* South Molton
Sportsmans Inn PH, Sandyway Cross
Poltimore Arms PH, North Molton

Mole's Chamber

Kinsford Gate

Sandyway Cross

Holywell Cross

North Molton

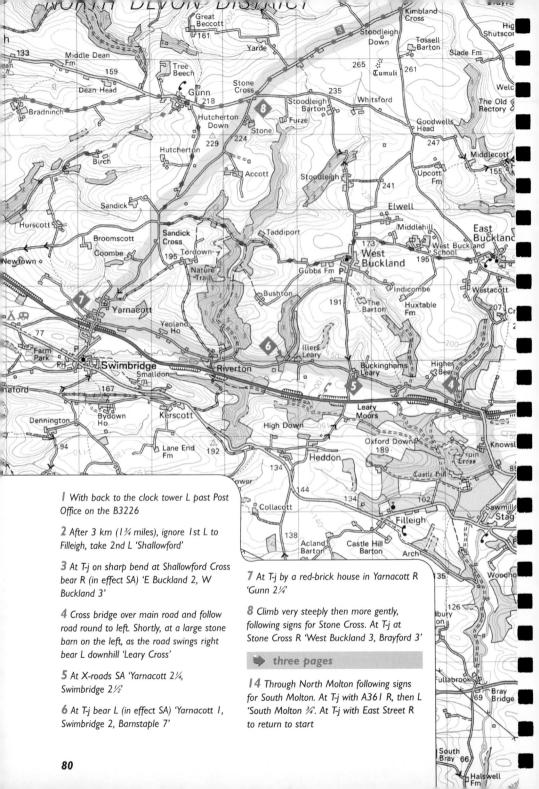

1 With back to the clock tower L past Post Office on the B3226

2 After 3 km (1¾ miles), ignore 1st L to Filleigh, take 2nd L 'Shallowford'

3 At T-j on sharp bend at Shallowford Cross bear R (in effect SA) 'E Buckland 2, W Buckland 3'

4 Cross bridge over main road and follow road round to left. Shortly, at a large stone barn on the left, as the road swings right bear L downhill 'Leary Cross'

5 At X-roads SA 'Yarnacott 2¼, Swimbridge 2½'

6 At T-j bear L (in effect SA) 'Yarnacott 1, Swimbridge 2, Barnstaple 7'

7 At T-j by a red-brick house in Yarnacott R 'Gunn 2¼'

8 Climb very steeply then more gently, following signs for Stone Cross. At T-j at Stone Cross R 'West Buckland 3, Brayford 3'

➡ **three pages**

14 Through North Molton following signs for South Molton. At T-j with A361 R, then L 'South Molton ¾'. At T-j with East Street R to return to start

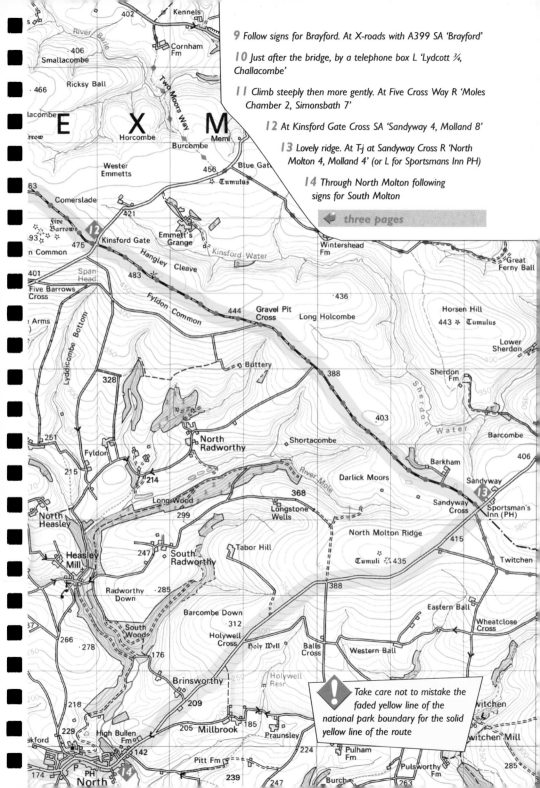

9 Follow signs for Brayford. At X-roads with A399 SA 'Brayford'

10 Just after the bridge, by a telephone box L 'Lydcott ¾, Challacombe'

11 Climb steeply then more gently. At Five Cross Way R 'Moles Chamber 2, Simonsbath 7'

12 At Kinsford Gate Cross SA 'Sandyway 4, Molland 8'

13 Lovely ridge. At T-j at Sandyway Cross R 'North Molton 4, Molland 4' (or L for Sportsmans Inn PH)

14 Through North Molton following signs for South Molton

← **three pages**

Take care not to mistake the faded yellow line of the national park boundary for the solid yellow line of the route

From Ottery St Mary to Exmouth and Budleigh, then back via the Otter valley

Start

The Volunteer Inn PH, Ottery St Mary

P Long-stay car park on road towards Talaton

Distance and grade

48 km (30 miles)

Easy/moderate

Terrain

Two main climbs: 91 m (300 ft) west from the Otter valley to Aylesbeare and 100 m (330 ft) from Exmouth to above Budleigh Salterton

Nearest railway

Exmouth

This is a reasonably easy ride; there is nowhere flat in Cornwall and Devon. Ottery St Mary is a busy little town that stages one of the most extraordinary bonfire nights you are ever likely to come across: men charge around the narrow, crowded streets with burning barrels on their shoulders. The ride starts and finishes by following the quiet lane along the Otter valley between Ottery St Mary and Fluxton. The route climbs out of the valley and heads southwest through Aylesbeare and Woodbury down to the sea at Exmouth, with fine views west across the estuary. You have to climb inland before rejoining the sea at the more genteel resort of Budleigh Salterton. The final third of the ride follows the delightful valley of the River Otter north through Otterton and Tipton St John and back to Ottery St Mary.

Ottery St Mary   Metcombe   Aylesbeare   Nine Oaks   Woodbury   Exmouth

Places of interest

A La Ronde, north of Exmouth 14/15
This unique, 16-sided house was built in 1796 by Misses Jane and Mary Parminter. It combines the features of a rustic cottage with the style of the Basilica of Ravenna. Its rooms and Gothic grottoes are arranged around an octagonal hall.

Refreshments

Lots of choice in Ottery St Mary
Halfway PH 🍴, Aylesbeare Inn PH, Aylesbeare
Diggers Rest PH 🍴🍴, Woodbury Salterton
Maltsters Arms PH, White Hart PH, Woodbury
Lots of choice in Exmouth
Salterton Arms PH 🍴 and others in
Budleigh Salterton
Kings Arms PH 🍴, Otterton
Golden Lion PH 🍴🍴, Tipton St John

Exmouth 16/17
Situated on the estuary of the River Exe, this pleasant town and small port is the oldest and one of the largest seaside resorts in Devon. There are beautiful views west to Haldon and Dartmoor.

Budleigh Salterton 21
During the 13th century, Budleigh Salterton was a salt-panning community supplying the local priory. There are several Georgian houses in the town and an art centre and museum at 27 Fore Street. Sir Walter Raleigh was born in a farmhouse nearby.

Otterton 24
Fine thatched cottages and a chestnut grove make this one of the most picturesque villages in the area. The restored Otterton Watermill is now a craft centre.

Bicton Park, near Otterton 24
Bicton Park comprises 50 acres of glorious gardens and parkland. There are glasshouses with fuchsias and geraniums and orchid houses.

Littleham   Budleigh Salterton   Otterton   Bridge End   Tipton St John

1 With back to Volunteer Inn PH L. At T-j with Canaan Way by St Anthony's Catholic Church L

2 Cross bridge and 1st L on Strawberry Way 'West Hill'. After 400 m (yd), at Salston Corner 1st L 'Fluxton 1½, Tipton St John 2'

3 Through Fluxton. Opposite telephone box by Angela Court Retirement Home R on Metcombe Vale 'Metcombe Vale ¼. West Hill 2¼, Aylesbeare 3'

4 At X-roads with B3180 at Tipton Cross SA 'Aylesbeare 1½'

5 At X-roads by Aylesbeare village hall, with white house ahead L 'Exmouth 8, Village Centre ¼'

6 1st R by Aylesbeare Inn PH onto Withen Lane 'Unsuitable for long vehicles'

7 At T-j at Withen Cross L. At X-roads with A3052 SA 'Unsuitable for long vehicles' (**Take care**)

8 After 800 m (½ mile) 1st R by triangle of grass

9 At T-j with breeze block barn ahead L (Brooklands Farm)

10 At T-j with Village Road L (in effect SA) 'Woodbury ¾'

11 In Woodbury, at X-roads with B3179 SA 'Lympstone 3, Exmouth 4'

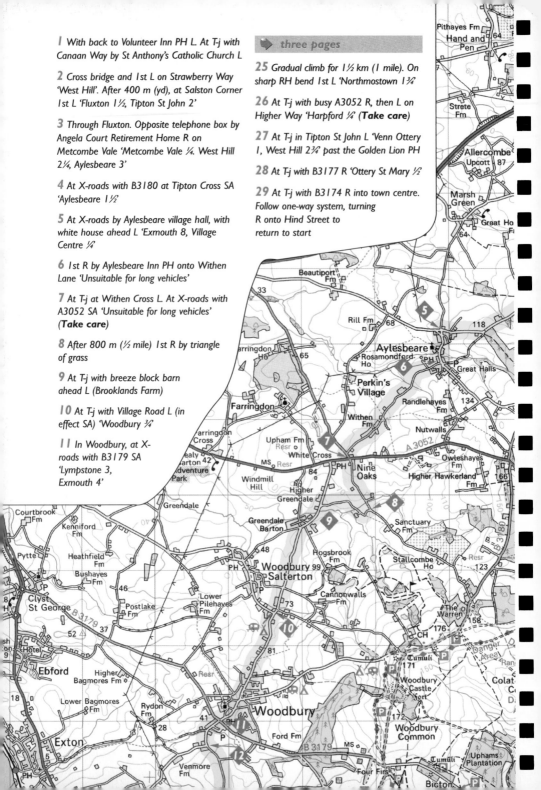

➤ **three pages**

25 Gradual climb for 1½ km (1 mile). On sharp RH bend 1st L 'Northmostown 1¾'

26 At T-j with busy A3052 R, then L on Higher Way 'Harpford ¼ (**Take care**)

27 At T-j in Tipton St John L 'Venn Ottery 1, West Hill 2¾' past the Golden Lion PH

28 At T-j with B3177 R 'Ottery St Mary ½'

29 At T-j with B3174 R into town centre. Follow one-way system, turning R onto Hind Street to return to start

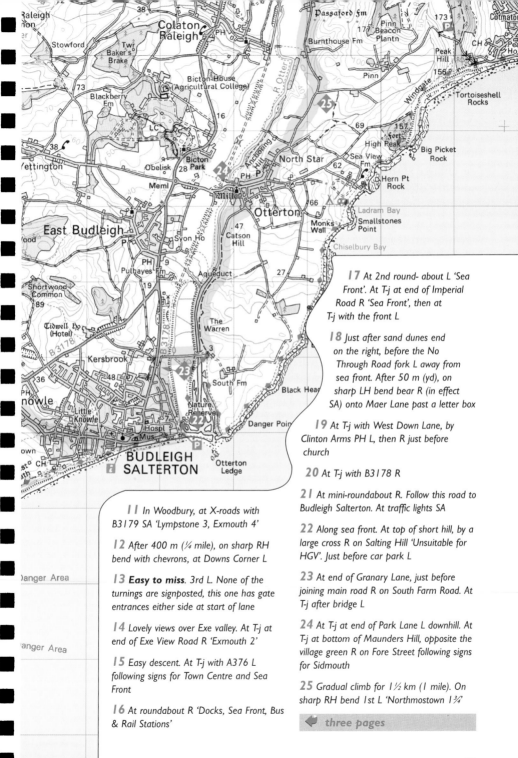

17 At 2nd round-about L 'Sea Front'. At T-j at end of Imperial Road R 'Sea Front', then at T-j with the front L

18 Just after sand dunes end on the right, before the No Through Road fork L away from sea front. After 50 m (yd), on sharp LH bend bear R (in effect SA) onto Maer Lane past a letter box

19 At T-j with West Down Lane, by Clinton Arms PH L, then R just before church

20 At T-j with B3178 R

21 At mini-roundabout R. Follow this road to Budleigh Salterton. At traffic lights SA

22 Along sea front. At top of short hill, by a large cross R on Salting Hill 'Unsuitable for HGV'. Just before car park L

23 At end of Granary Lane, just before joining main road R on South Farm Road. At T-j after bridge L

24 At T-j at end of Park Lane L downhill. At T-j at bottom of Maunders Hill, opposite the village green R on Fore Street following signs for Sidmouth

25 Gradual climb for 1½ km (1 mile). On sharp RH bend 1st L 'Northmostown 1¾'

◀ three pages

11 In Woodbury, at X-roads with B3179 SA 'Lympstone 3, Exmouth 4'

12 After 400 m (¼ mile), on sharp RH bend with chevrons, at Downs Corner L

13 **Easy to miss**. 3rd L. None of the turnings are signposted, this one has gate entrances either side at start of lane

14 Lovely views over Exe valley. At T-j at end of Exe View Road R 'Exmouth 2'

15 Easy descent. At T-j with A376 L following signs for Town Centre and Sea Front

16 At roundabout R 'Docks, Sea Front, Bus & Rail Stations'

From Truro into the Poldice valley

Start

The Royal Hotel,
Lemon Quay, Truro

P Long-stay car park
on the B3284
Perranporth Road

20 Distance and grade

32 km (20 miles)
Moderate

Nearest railway

Truro

Cornwall is singularly ill-supplied with quality off-road tracks; there are relatively few bridleways and these frequently stop or change status in the middle of nowhere and are often poorly maintained. This route is a mixture of quiet lanes and short sections of old tracks once used by the mining industry. The ride heads south from Truro along lanes through Porth Kea and Cowlands to Feock. A pleasant section along the Restronguet Creek takes you to Devoran, location of the fine Old Quay Inn. The A39 seems to be the border marking the start of the old mining area. Pick your way amongst the lanes and tracks heading northwest to the top of the Poldice valley. The local authority has made efforts to promote leisure use of this old industrial landscape, so more signposted trails are likely to appear in the next few years. Climbing out of the Poldice valley past Wheal Baddon and Wheal Jane mines, a last off-road section over Carrine Common leads to the lane that ends at the County Hall in Truro.

Truro   Porth Kea   Cowlands   Feock   Devoran   Perranwell Station

Terrain

Several climbs of between 45 and 61 m (150 and 200 ft) between Truro and the estuary. 106 m (350 ft) climb from Bissoe past Wheal Jane towards Truro

Refreshments

*Lots of choice in **Truro**
Old Quay Inn PH 🍴, **Devoran**
Cornish Arms PH, **Frogpool***

Places of interest

Feock 8

The village of Feock had one prosperous fling during the Industrial Revolution, when its tin mines flourished and a smelting plant roared away at Penpol, a mile to the north. Free-spending miners, sailors and rail gangers filled the area. The industry died out in the early 1900s and Feock returned to its agricultural ways.

Chacewater *(3 km (2 miles) north of Crofthandy) 21*

James Watt installed his first pumping engine at Wheal Busy copper mine in 1777. The engine house, smithy and cottage are still in reasonable repair.

Crofthandy

Hale Mills

Bissoe

Penweathers

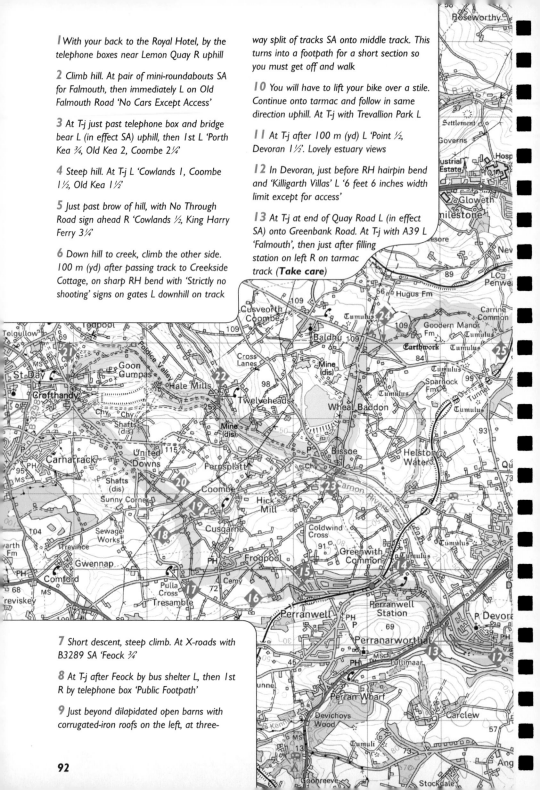

1 With your back to the Royal Hotel, by the telephone boxes near Lemon Quay R uphill

2 Climb hill. At pair of mini-roundabouts SA for Falmouth, then immediately L on Old Falmouth Road 'No Cars Except Access'

3 At T-j just past telephone box and bridge bear L (in effect SA) uphill, then 1st L 'Porth Kea ¾, Old Kea 2, Coombe 2¼'

4 Steep hill. At T-j L 'Cowlands 1, Coombe 1½, Old Kea 1½'

5 Just past brow of hill, with No Through Road sign ahead R 'Cowlands ½, King Harry Ferry 3¼'

6 Down hill to creek, climb the other side. 100 m (yd) after passing track to Creekside Cottage, on sharp RH bend with 'Strictly no shooting' signs on gates L downhill on track

7 Short descent, steep climb. At X-roads with B3289 SA 'Feock ¾'

8 At T-j after Feock by bus shelter L, then 1st R by telephone box 'Public Footpath'

9 Just beyond dilapidated open barns with corrugated-iron roofs on the left, at three-way split of tracks SA onto middle track. This turns into a footpath for a short section so you must get off and walk

10 You will have to lift your bike over a stile. Continue onto tarmac and follow in same direction uphill. At T-j with Trevallion Park L

11 At T-j after 100 m (yd) L 'Point ½, Devoran 1½'. Lovely estuary views

12 In Devoran, just before RH hairpin bend and 'Killigarth Villas' L '6 feet 6 inches width limit except for access'

13 At T-j at end of Quay Road L (in effect SA) onto Greenbank Road. At T-j with A39 L 'Falmouth', then just after filling station on left R on tarmac track (**Take care**)

14 Tarmac turns to stony track. At fork in clearing, by a house called 'Newlands' on the right bear R to continue on stony track (not tarmac). After 100 m (yd) at X-roads SA 'Grenna Lane ¼, Greenwith Cross ½'

15 Follow road over railway bridge and round to the left. Shortly after offset X-roads, on sharp RH bend by Woodbine Cottage bear L (in effect SA) 'Public Bridleway', then at fork after 50 m (yd) R

16 At T-j with tarmac (post box and farm on left) R uphill. At T-j with road and on bend L

17 20 m (yd) after passing Trelawney housing estate on right R on track 'No vehicular access to playing field'

18 At X-roads with road SA onto track through ford. At T-j by large, white, stone house on left R uphill

19 At T-j with white stone house on right (Rose Cottage) L, then R on track

20 At offset X-roads of tracks SA. At road R on United Downs 'Carharrack 1, Crofthandy 1, Chacewater 3'

21 In Crofthandy, on sharp LH bend by Methodist Church bear R (in effect SA) onto Higher Goon Gumpas Lane. After 30 m (yd) fork R by telegraph pole, then L by gate

22 Instructions are difficult for this section as there are many tracks and more are being created. Aim towards the bottom of the valley continuing in the same direction. Good tracks in amongst the industrial wasteland. At tarmac SA for 50 m (yd), then L as soon as possible to rejoin track along the valley

23 Eventually rejoin tarmac, turn L. At X-roads in Bissoe, shortly after Post Office on left L 'Wheal Jane ½'

24 At T-j R 'Carnon Downs 2½, Devoran 4, Falmouth 10'. After 200 m (yd) 2nd track L along line of telegraph poles 'No dumping'. After 400 m (¼ mile) at fork bear L following telegraph poles

25 Follow main, stony track to road, turn L

26 At X-roads with A390 dismount to cross this busy road and go SA onto Chapel Hill. At T-j R onto Kenwyn Street

27 At T-j at the end of Charles Street L to return to start

2 Granite tracks over Dartmoor south from Princetown to Burrator Reservoir

Start

Between the Devils Elbow PH and the Plume of Feathers PH, Princetown

P Follow signs

Distance and grade

26 km (16 miles)

Moderate

Terrain

Two main climbs, both on road: 152 m (500 ft) from the dam at Burrator to the car park on the B3212 and 183 m (600 ft) from Merrivale back to Princetown

Nearest railway

Plymouth, 14 km (9 miles) south of Yelverton

This ride shows the various faces of Dartmoor. The first part is over bleak, heather-covered peat and granite moorland. The middle section passes through the woods surrounding Burrator Reservoir and offers a diversion to the attractive village and pub at Meavy. Further on is the delightful Walkham River valley. Starting from Princetown, the ride climbs towards the distinctive rocky outcrop of South Hessary Tor. It is quite a challenge to see how much of this you can ride without getting off, but if this does not appeal, there is a parallel road to the east that will bring you to almost the same spot. A 5 km (3 mile) descent, at times technical, drops you near the edge of Burrator Reservoir. You go round three sides of this before bearing left uphill towards Sharpitor. A short section on the Princetown road leads to a cross-country descent into the beautiful Walkham River valley. This Tolkienesque landscape ends at the main Tavistock-Princetown road near Merrivale, from which point you have a 5½ km (3½ mile) road climb back to Princetown.

Princetown

Sheepstor

Burrator Reservoir

Princetown 1

Princetown is most famous for its high-security prison. The first prison was founded here in 1806 by Sir Martin Pailthorpe and was used for French prisoners taken in the Napoleonic Wars. It became a convict prison in 1850. Many of the roads across the remote parts of the moor were built by forced labour.

Near Hucken Tor, south of Merrivale

Meavy *(just off the route near Sheepstor)* 6 Meavy is a tiny, timeless village in a fold of the moor. The shattered remains of a leaning oak, said to be the last of Devon's 'dancing trees', was a focal point for pagan rites to the mythological figure Olred. A Tudor house adjoining the church once belonged to the Drake family.

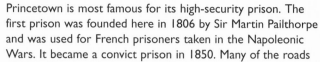
Lots of choice in **Princetown**
Royal Oak PH 🍺, *off the route at* **Meavy**
Dartmoor Inn PH 🍺, **Merrivale**

Routrundle

Daveytown

Merrivale

Rundlestone

1 Take the lane/track between the two pubs onto the moor. Follow this for almost 3 km (2 miles). You climb alongside a wall for a while

2 Shortly after a boundary stone shaped like an obelisk, at a major X-roads of tracks R. This is an excellent descent

3 After 3 km (2 miles), at fork of tracks with pine trees on your right bear L downhill

4 At T-j with the road, with a bridge ahead L. You will soon have views across Burrator Reservoir

5 At next T-j, with Sheepstor Church away to your left R

6 Cross over dam and turn R (or L then first L for Meavy and pub). After 800 m (½ mile), shortly after green barn on your right L uphill

7 At T-j with B3212 R 'Princetown'. After climbing, then descending, at a car park on your left at the bottom of a small hill, before reaching a conifer plantation on your right turn L through car park onto bridleway. The track is at first indistinct but soon crosses a dismantled railway

8 Cross the old railway and head downhill towards a wooden gate and building. Follow this for almost 1½ km (1 mile)

9 At tarmac L, then at Criptor Cross R onto No Through Road 'Daveytown'

10 At the end of the tarmac by Daveytown SA 'Public Bridleway. Merrivale'

11 Lovely wooded section with fine views to the left. Track improves near farm. At T-j with road R

12 After 3 km (2 miles), at Rundlestone Cross, 1st road R 'Princetown' to return to start

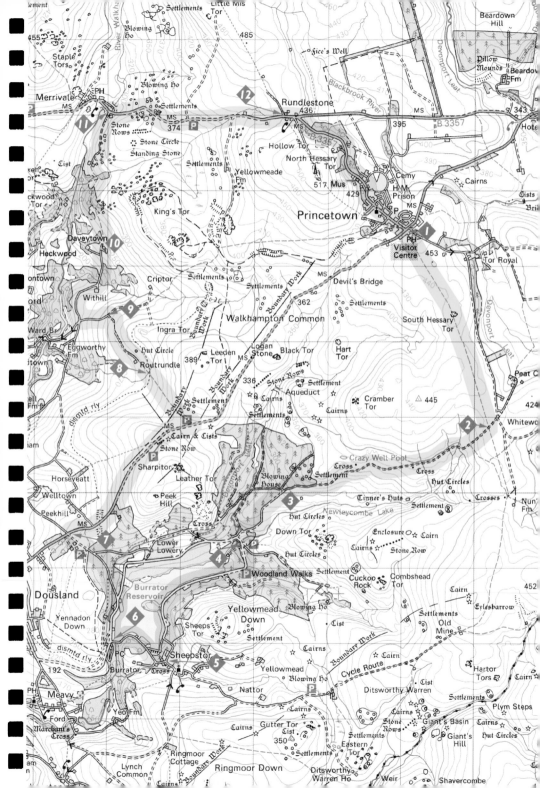

3 To Grimspound and Hound Tor from North Bovey

Start

Car park opposite church in North Bovey, 5 km (3 miles) southwest of Moretonhampstead

P As above

Distance and grade

29 km (18 miles)

Strenuous

Nearest railway

Yeoford, 16 km (10 miles) north of North Bovey or Newton Abbot, 16 km (10 miles) southwest of Trendlebere Down

This ride explores eastern Dartmoor, visiting the atmospheric stone circle of Grimspound and the weird crags of Hound Tor, both perhaps inspiration for Sir Arthur Conan Doyle's *The Hound of the Baskervilles*. The ride is a mixture of steep road and off-road climbs; the scenery is always spectacular, but at times the going is rough enough to necessitate walking for short sections. The ride starts from North Bovey and if you time your ride correctly, you can return for refreshments at the excellent village pub. You are almost immediately faced with the steepest road climb of the ride. A short descent, followed by a much longer, off-road climb, past the vast granite blocks of West Coombe Farm, take you up to the moor. You have climbed to 488 m (1600 ft) and the area is fairly exposed so be prepared with compass and waterproofs for mist, fog, rain and winds. Unfortunately, there is no legal route from Hookney Tor to Grimspound, so you must lose height to the road, then climb again to the stone circle. The descent beyond Grimspound is reasonably fine. The countryside past Greator Rocks is characterized by glades, boulders and rushing streams; you will have to walk parts of this. A steep climb precedes a tough descent alongside the forest. The route meanders through Water and Foxworthy, goes up to the road at Barnecourt and then back to North Bovey.

North Bovey   Canna Park   Grimspound   Hound Tor

Terrain

Three main climbs, all in the first half of the ride: a very steep road climb of 106 m (350 ft) at the start from North Bovey, 204 m (670 ft) from Canna Park to Hookney Tor (will involve pushing) and 82 m (270 ft) from the road to above Grimspound. There are several other short climbs that will involve some pushing

Refreshments

Grimspound

Places of interest

North Bovey 1
A medieval stone cross stands on the edge of the green in this lovingly preserved Dartmoor village. Thatched granite cottages, many over 200 years old, and the 13th-century Ring of Bells Inn flank the green and form an attractive group by the 13th-century church.

Grimspound 4
This is a fine example of a Bronze Age shepherd settlement. It consists of 24 small hut circles in a walled enclosure with a paved entrance.

Hound Tor 7
The wind, gusting through the crags and crevices of Hound Tor, sets up a weird howling like a pack of hounds baying. Some say that the tor gave Sir Arthur Conan Doyle the idea for his chilling story *The Hound of the Baskervilles*. The remains of a medieval village can be traced close to the tor. A better climate in the Bronze Age made Dartmoor sites at over 300 m (1000 ft) above sea level habitable; in some cases they remained inhabited until the 14th century.

Becka Falls 10/11
The clear brook water at Becka Falls tumble 21 m (70 ft) over a jumble of boulders forming tree-fringed pools.

Leighon · Trendlebere Down · Water · Manaton · Foxworthy · Barnecourt

1 From car park L downhill. 1st R 'Princetown'. After 200 m (yd) 1st L over bridge 'Princetown'

2 Very steep climb. At X-roads SA onto No Through Road 'Hookner Coombe'. Cross bridge. Ignore right turn to Shapley

3 At farm at West Combe SA 'Bridlepath to moor'. As concrete track swings right bear L (in effect SA). Steeply up RH side of the valley to a gate in the stone wall on the horizon. Through gate and L alongside wall. Continue in same direction climbing then descending, keeping the wall on your left

4 At T-j with road L. After 800 m (½ mile), just before RH hairpin bend L uphill on rough track heading up the valley to the large stone compound of Grimspound

5 Through the stone circle, keeping to main track, ignoring one right and one left turn. Aim for RH edge of wood. Magnificent, open descent to road

6 At T-j with road L, then R 'Hound Tor via Jay's Grave and Hayne Down 4 km (2½ miles). Hayne Down for Manaton'

7 At T-j with road R. At junction of roads head towards RH side of rocks that form Hound Tor (no obvious track) and contour L round the back of the tor. Aim for the furthest LH outcrop of rocks of Greator, where rocks and wood meet

8 Through wooden gate 'Leighon via Haytor Down'. Steep descent to cross stream. Follow stone wall on your left and signs to 'Leighon'

9 At junction of tracks SA uphill 'Upper Terrace Drive'

10 At road R, then after 800 m (½ mile), at a stone wall at edge of wood L 'Trendlebere Down and County Road'. Follow edge of wood or track running parallel slightly away from wood

11 At T-j with road L

12 After 3 km (2 miles), in Manaton (Freeland), just before Kestor Inn PH 1st road R 'Water'. At T-j by three-way wooden signpost L 'Bovey valley. Lustleigh. Manaton'. After 50 m (yd) bear R, then just before farm L 'Bridlepath only, no vehicles'

13 After 200 m (yd), at junction of tracks L 'Manaton indirect and Horsham'. Keep following signs for Manaton. After 800 m (½ mile), at the start of tarmac next to a black, corrugated-iron shed L on track

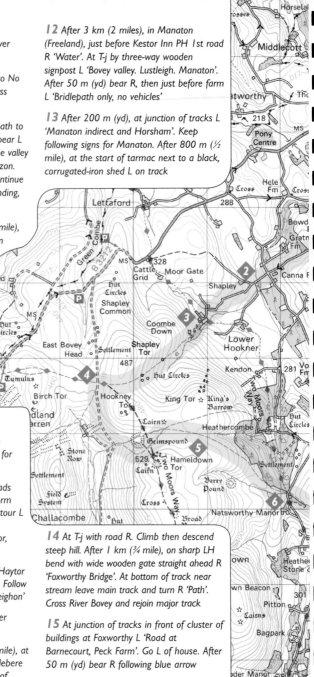

14 At T-j with road R. Climb then descend steep hill. After 1 km (¾ mile), on sharp LH bend with wide wooden gate straight ahead R 'Foxworthy Bridge'. At bottom of track near stream leave main track and turn R 'Path'. Cross River Bovey and rejoin major track

15 At junction of tracks in front of cluster of buildings at Foxworthy L 'Road at Barnecourt, Peck Farm'. Go L of house. After 50 m (yd) bear R following blue arrow

16 At junction with concrete path L (in effect SA). At road R, then 1st L down No Through Road to return to start

4 ▸ Southwest from Okehampton to Meldon Reservoir and Sourton Tors

Start

White Hart Hotel,
High Street,
Okehampton

P Long-stay car park
on Market Street

Distance and grade

21 km (13 miles)
Moderate

Terrain

Two main climbs:
204 m (670 ft) from
Okehampton to just
beneath Sourton Tors
and 106 m (350 ft) to
the mast above
Thorndon Cross

Nearest railway

Copplestone, 24 km
(15 miles) east of
Okehampton

The first half of this ride hugs the northern edge of Dartmoor and the second half follows quiet lanes and old county roads through small farming communities. The ride starts by crossing the Okehampton Golf Course. A short distance after this, you may be surprised to come across a top quality tarmac road where none is shown on the map: this is used by the lorries that trundle to and from the stone quarries at Meldon. You soon pass under the soaring viaduct that used to carry the railway. A climb takes you through woodland to the dam at the end of the Meldon Reservoir. Although there is a bridleway signposted straight ahead, it is better to turn right and follow a parallel bridleway between stone walls up to the moor. This heads towards Sourton Tors, passing over the earth ridges once owned by the Sourton Ice Works. The views from here are spectacular. A fast descent brings you out opposite the Highwayman Inn. Try to time your ride so that you arrive during opening hours; it is worth having a look around the inside of this bizarre building. From here onwards, the route follows quiet lanes and county roads, with the exception of a short stretch on the A3079, and finishes with a fine, fast descent back into Okehampton.

Okehampton   Meldon   South Down   Sourton Tors   Sourton   Forda

Sourton Tors 8

In the late 19th century, the cool springs of Sourton Tors were used by the Sourton Ice Works to produce large blocks of ice in shallow ponds during the winter. These were transported to Plymouth in spring and early summer – a slow journey by horse and cart during which much of the product melted away. The ice left was used in food preservation, particularly for fish. Undulations in the land mark the site of these ponds.

Refreshments

Lots of choice in **Okehampton**
Highwayman PH ❤❤, **Sourton**

The Highwayman Inn, Sourton 11

The sheer eccentricity of this pub's remarkable design will leave you astounded: the porch (a mock nobleman's carriage) leads into a warren of dimly lit stonework and flagstone-floored burrows and alcoves.

The Highwayman Inn, Sourton

Week Farm
Cowsen Down
Thorndon Cross
Yelland

1 With back to White Hart Hotel R on George Street 'Okehampton Camp'. 20 m (yd) after passing Post Office R on Station Road 'Okehampton Camp 1'

2 Go past telephone box then Brandize Park Road on the left. After 100 m (yd) R 'To the Golf Club'

3 Follow signs 'Bridleway Meldon'. As lane swings left uphill towards club house bear R onto track 'Bridlepath. Beware Golf Balls'

4 Exit golf course via gate. Continue in same direction along RH field-edge following wooden signposts. Through farm. At T-j with tarmac L on bridge over A30

5 Follow lane (beware quarry lorries) until passing under vast iron bridge. Bear R on track 'Public Bridleway. Meldon Reservoir'. Cross bridge over river and turn L uphill

6 At X-roads of tracks near dam R onto tarmac 'Bridlepath to Meldon'. Through gate, down hill. At T-j near old railway bridge L onto No Through Road 'To Bridlepaths to the Moor'

7 As tarmac swings left towards Higher Bowden House SA onto track. Through gate onto grassy track along RH field-edge. Through next gate onto continuation of track enclosed between stone walls

8 Once beyond enclosed track, aim for the rocky outcrop at the top of Sourton Tors. Follow the wall on your left until shortly before it bears away sharply to the left (at tall standing stone)

9 Continue on grassy track towards tor for 300 m (yd) until reaching pair of standing stones. After 50 m (yd) R on grassy track contouring beneath earthwork embankments

10 Follow this track as it turns from grass to stone and bears R downhill to church at Sourton

11 At X-roads with A386, by public house SA onto lane

12 At X-roads with the old A30 SA 'Unsuitable for motors'

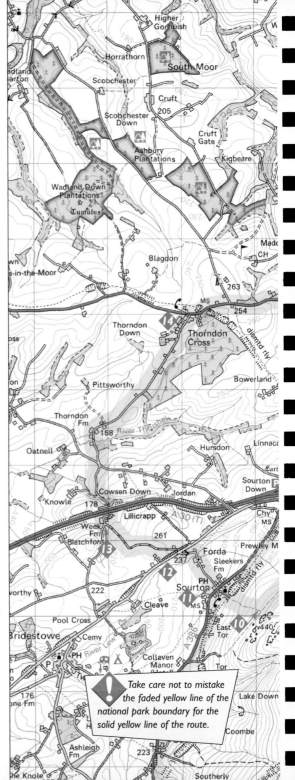

Take care not to mistake the faded yellow line of the national park boundary for the solid yellow line of the route.

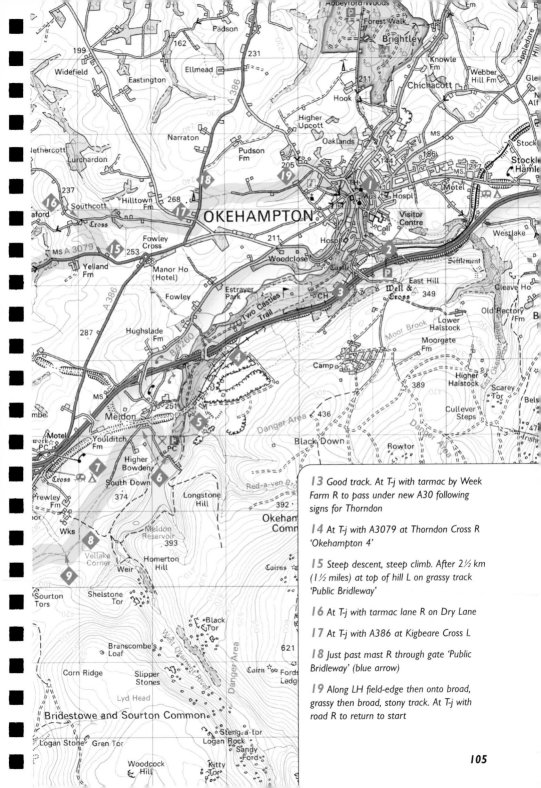

13 Good track. At T-j with tarmac by Week Farm R to pass under new A30 following signs for Thorndon

14 At T-j with A3079 at Thorndon Cross R 'Okehampton 4'

15 Steep descent, steep climb. After 2½ km (1½ miles) at top of hill L on grassy track 'Public Bridleway'

16 At T-j with tarmac lane R on Dry Lane

17 At T-j with A386 at Kigbeare Cross L

18 Just past mast R through gate 'Public Bridleway' (blue arrow)

19 Along LH field-edge then onto broad, grassy then broad, stony track. At T-j with road R to return to start

5 South from Okehampton onto highest Dartmoor

Start

The White Hart Hotel, High Street, Okehampton

🅿 Long-stay car park on Market Street

Distance and grade

21 km (13 miles)
27 km (17 miles) with detour to Hangingstone Hill)

🏃🏃🏃 Moderate

Nearest railway

Copplestone, 24 km (15 miles) east of Okehampton

*T*he statistics of this ride make it seem a lot harder than it really is: a steady climb of 427 m (1400 ft) sounds somewhat daunting. It is not so bad, however, when you realize that most of the climb is either on tarmac or on good, broad, stone-based tracks that follow a relatively steady gradient. The ride makes use of the Okehampton Army Firing Range tracks, so do not be alarmed if you come across some heavily armed soldiers. It has the advantage of being a truly all-year-round track (except, perhaps, for winter snow). It is worth waiting for a fine day in order to appreciate the views from the top, particularly if you wish to go to Hangingstone Hill. The ride starts in Okehampton and climbs towards the castle. This is followed by a delightful flat section next to the old railway track and above the valley formed by the East Okement River. After this, you dive under and over railway, river and road bridges and then climb towards Belstone, with its fine inn. From here, you are onto the moor itself. The East Okement River is crossed with minimum height loss and a couple of miles of almost flat cycling follow. Appreciate the views of North Devon that open up behind you. The gradient steepens and you may wish to push on to Hangingstone Hill for a true 'Roof of Devon' experience. Alternatively, if you have had enough climbing, take stock of your surroundings as they might be somewhat blurred on the 8 km (5 mile) descent back to Okehampton!

Okehampton

Stockley Hamlet

Belstone

Okement Hill

Okehampton

 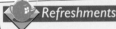
Places of interest

Okehampton 1

This small market town, the life of which has been changed dramatically by the building of the A30 bypass, boasts of a handsome 17th-century Town Hall and an old three-storey mill housing the Museum of Dartmoor Life. The parish church has windows by the Victorian artist William Morris.

Okehampton Castle 1

Set high on a knoll above the river, Okehampton Castle was built by the Sherriff of Devon shortly after the Norman Conquest. Of the surviving castle ruins, only the keep is Norman, the rest dates from the early 14th century. The ruins have attracted many artists, including Turner. They are also haunted: Lady Howard, who murdered at least two of her four husbands, is said to expiate her crimes by travelling nightly between Tavistock and Okehampton in a coach made of her husbands' bones. The carriage stops at the castle mound, where she picks a single blade of grass before returning to Tavistock; not until the mound is bare will she be allowed to rest.

Museum of Water Power

6½ km (4 miles) east of Okehampton 1
Finch Foundry was a 19th-century water-powered factory producing sickles, scythes and shovels. It is now a museum with working waterwheels driving ancient machinery.

Hangingstone Hill

Okement Hill

Okehampton Camp

1 With back to White Hart Hotel R on George Street 'Okehampton Camp'. 20 m (yd) after passing Post Office R on Station Road 'Okehampton Camp 1'

2 1st L by St Boniface Catholic Church 'DTFS Centre ¼'. Just before railway viaduct, opposite tall metal railings on the right bear L onto track 'Bridlepath to Father Ford'

3 At junction of tracks underneath railway viaduct L 'Okehampton via Ball Hill'. Cross bridge and go back under railway bridge on other side of river, then R through gate onto road

4 At T-j R, then 1st R 'Tor Down 3/4' to go under the railway viaduct a third time

5 Climb steeply to Belstone. At T-j in Belstone R on No Through Road past Tor Cottage

6 Beautiful track, climbing then descending to cross river. Fork L uphill soon after crossing river. At tarmac L

7 If you wish to go up to Hangingstone Hill (worth it on days with excellent visibility), just after reaching highest point on tarmac road by stone army shelter, take the 1st track L as it drops then climbs on rough surface to the stone building at the top. If you do not wish to go to Hangingstone Hill, do not leave tarmac track but follow it as it swings back round towards the north

8 Follow this wonderful descent for 8 km (5 miles) back to Okehampton

9 At bottom of Station Road L to return to start

Take care not to mistake the faded yellow line of the national park boundary for the solid yellow line of the route.

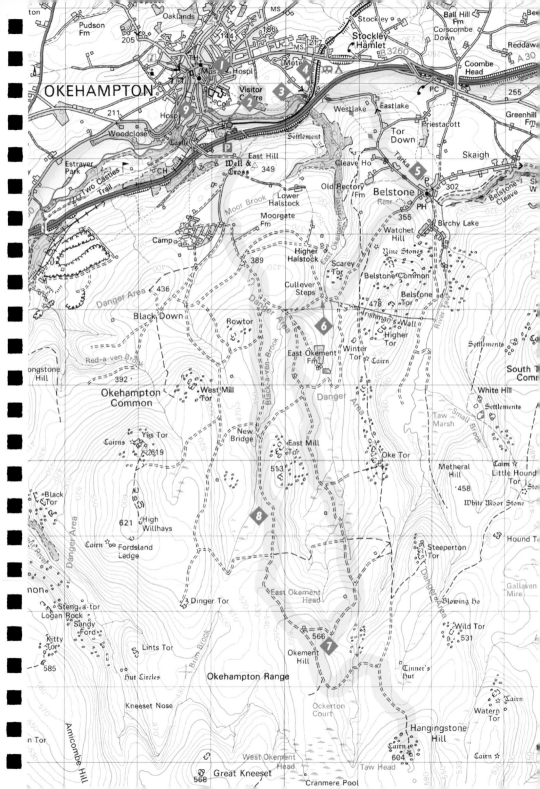

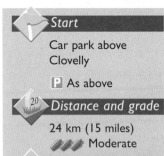

Clovelly west to Hartland Point

Hartland Point is undoubtedly the most impressive feature of this ride: the mighty cliff rises 99 m (325 ft) from the sea, squarely facing the worst of the Atlantic gales. The ride starts from Clovelly, too pretty by far for some people's taste, and now subject to a visitors' charge. This is soon left behind as you plunge into woodland and steep valleys between Clovelly Church and Brownsham. Quiet lanes take you from Brownsham to Hartland Point; a visit is absolutely essential for fans of the sea and dramatic landscapes. South from here, lies a series of valleys that you have to cross in quick succession. After the steepest of these, you emerge in Stoke and have a choice of turning right towards Hartland Quay and the Hotel, left towards the handsome village of Hartland with its choice of pubs, or continuing straight ahead on the route towards Wargery. The return to Clovelly is predominantly on narrow lanes with high hedgerows, interspersed with the odd off-road section on old county roads.

Start

Car park above Clovelly

P As above

Distance and grade

24 km (15 miles)

Moderate

Terrain

Two main climbs: 122 m (400 ft) from the woods to the west of Clovelly and 106 m (350 ft) to the B3248 above Clovelly; also several short, steep climbs south of Hartland Point.

Nearest railway

Barnstaple, 34 km (21 miles) east of the route

Clovelly

Brownsham

Titchberry

Blegberry

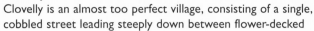

Clovelly 1

Clovelly is an almost too perfect village, consisting of a single, cobbled street leading steeply down between flower-decked cottages to a small, curving quay. Transport is on foot and there is now a charge for visiting the village. It is very popular in the holiday season.

Near Hartland Point

Hartland Point 8

Known to the Romans as the 'Promontory of Hercules', Hartland Point is a sheer 99 m (325 ft) cliff on a coastline battered by Atlantic gales. The lighthouse is the most powerful on the British coast.

Hartland Quay *(just off the route)* 12

At the foot of the fearsome cliffs is a 16th-century harbour that was once used by smugglers.

Hartland Abbey *(just off the route)* 12

This abbey dates from the 12th century but was greatly added to in later periods. It was given by Henry VIII to William Abbott in 1546 and is still owned by the same family.

Hartland *(3 km (2 miles) off the route)* 12 Hartland is a pretty village of stone and slate cottages. The clock above the chapel door is the oldest in North Devon.

Refreshments

Lots of choice in Clovelly
Hartland Quay Hotel, *Hartland Quay*
Anchor PH, Kings Arms PH, Hart Inn PH, *just off the route in* Hartland

Stoke · Wargery · Leigh · Farford · Natcott · Sierra

1 From Car Park, return to road and turn L. After 800 m (½ mile), on sharp LH bend R through gates 'Clovelly Parish Church'

2 Follow road round 'Court Farm, Sawmills. Public Bridleway' to end of tarmac. Through farm on stony track in same direction along upper LH edge of field

3 At large, round water tank at end of field R downhill with hedgerow to your left, then L through 1st gate 'Public Bridleway'. Follow lower RH field-edge into wood

4 Deep, sunken, eroded track. At T-j with better track L for 50 m (yd), then R 'Public Bridleway'

5 Through woods climbing gently. At tarmac at Lower Brownsham Farm L uphill following signs for Hartland Point

6 At T-j at Brownsham Cross R 'Hartland Point and Lighthouse 3'

7 At X-roads at Youltree Cross R 'Hartland Point and Lighthouse 2¼'

8 Follow to Hartland Point. At T-j beyond car park attendant's booth R to Hartland Point for magnificent and dramatic sea views. Return to this point and continue SA

9 Go through farm. After 400 m (¼ mile) 1st L to cross stream via wicket gate (blue arrow). A steady push, at top the track improves

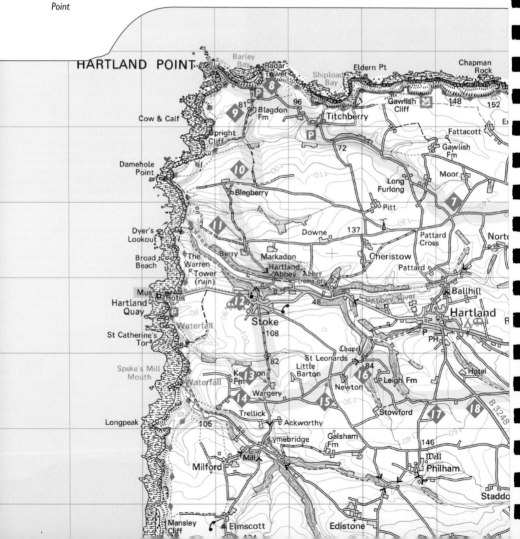

10 At tarmac R, then just before barn L on broad, stony track. Descend then another push (may be muddy)

11 At tarmac bear R (in effect SA) towards church 'Unsuitable for motors'

12 Steep down then up. In Stoke L, then R by Rose Cottage

13 Tarmac lane turns to stone track. At T-j with tarmac at Wargery Farm R

14 At X-roads at Kernstone Cross L 'Hartland, Bideford'

15 At offset X-roads at Newton Cross L, then R 'Public Footpath to Hartland Point'

16 At bottom of hill at Cuckoo Cottage bear R on concrete track. Through farm. At X-roads of tracks with three gates ahead L (no gate)

17 At road L, then after 50 m (yd) on LH bend R (NS)

18 At X-roads with B3248 SA (NS)

19 At T-j L (NS). Through Natcott. After 800 m (½ mile), opposite 1st turning to left R on track

20 At T-j with tarmac L. At fork after 400 m (¼ mile) R. At T-j with B3248 R

21 After 400 m (¼ mile) on sharp RH bend at Clarks Corner Cross L

22 At T-j with B3237 L 'Clovelly' to return to start

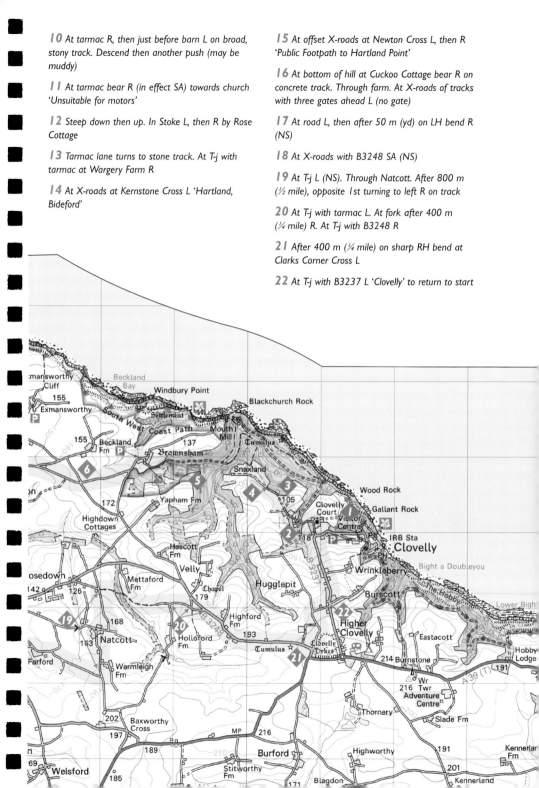

7 In and out of the Yeo valley north of Barnstaple

Start

The Museum of North Devon, Barnstaple

P Follow signs for long-stay car parks

20 Distance and grade

30 km (19 miles)

Strenuous

Terrain

Four main climbs: 213 m (700 ft) from Barnstaple to Gunn, 106 m (350 ft) between Stoke Rivers and Goodleigh, 91 m (300 ft) from the River Yeo to the A39 and 70 m (230 ft) from Bradiford Water to Springfield Cross

Nearest railway

Barnstaple

There are three main designated cycle trails on dismantled railways in Devon and Cornwall: the Camel Trail, which runs through Padstow and Wadebridge; the Plym Valley Route north from Plymouth; and the Tarka Trail, which runs south from Barnstaple to Petrockstowe and west to Braunton. These all provide safe and easy cycling. This ride uses the Tarka Trail between Ashford and Barnstaple along the north bank of the Taw estuary. The ride heads east out of Barnstaple, soon joins quiet lanes and then climbs steeply on a wooded track to Birch and on to Gunn. The last section can be muddy, so you will sometimes have to push. Stoke Rivers is little more than a collection of farmhouses around the church. You are now at the start of one of the best descents of the ride – the old county road that leads to Goodleigh. A long descent is followed by a long climb, the first part of which is fairly steep. If you are prepared to lose some height, there is a pub and a shop in Goodleigh. A second, fast descent takes you to the bridge over the River Yeo. The steep climb to the A39 should bring you out opposite another old county road. This is totally overgrown, so a short diversion on the A39 is required to regain this lane near the fish farm. A short, tarmac section through Ashford takes you down to the Taw estuary, with its wide views, and to the Tarka Trail, which you follow back to Barnstaple. If you wish to extend the ride, ignore the turning to Ashford, continue west to Braunton and join the Tarka Trail at its start.

Barnstaple   Landkey   Birch   Gunn   Stoke Rivers

Barnstaple 1

Once a harbour on the estuary of the River Taw and an ancient trading centre, Barnstaple is North Devon's major market town. Its lovely old bridge, 213 m (700 ft) long with 16 pointed arches, dates from the 15th century. The wool trade brought prosperity to Barnstaple in the 18th century and its predominantly Georgian architecture reflects this period of growth. The partly 14th-century parish church has a twisted wooden spire.

Marwood Hill (just off the route) 17

Roses and arum lilies compete with Australasian exotica in a garden created by damming a stream to form a series of lakes.

 Refreshments

Corner House PH 🍺 and others in Barnstaple
New Inn PH, Goodleigh
Sweets and tea, Blakewell Fisheries

The Yeo Valley north of Goodleigh

Goodleigh
Northleigh

Burridge

Blakewell

Ashford

1 From clocktower next to the Museum of North Devon head away from museum on road signposted 'Newport'

2 Follow this road in same direction. At X-roads by Rose and Crown PH SA

3 After 3 km (2 miles) at T-j L 'Barnstaple, Taunton A361', then 1st R onto Birch Road 'Harford ¾, Acland 1, Goodleigh 2'

4 After 1 km (¾ mile), at the bottom of a gentle hill L through bridge under the main road 'Hurscott 1¼, Birch 1½, Gunn 3', then SA onto No Through Road

5 At cluster of buildings at top of long climb on sealed surface, as track bears sharp right continue SA through gate along RH field-edge and follow in the same direction

6 A short, enclosed, muddy section in the wood soon improves and bears L through hedgerow (blue arrow)

7 At T-j with better track by farm fork R. Follow through farm onto tarmac. At T-j by 'Rustic Cottage' R

8 At T-j with more major road by Gunn Cottage R. Ignore 1st left over cattle grid. After 1½ km (1 mile) at Yarde Cross L 'Stoke Rivers'

9 At T-j in Stoke Rivers L. Just past telephone box on the right 1st L 'Goodleigh unsuitable for motors'. Stay close to farm buildings on your right

10 Superb descent. Tough then easier climb. At tarmac in Goodleigh 1st R (or L for New Inn PH) up small narrow lane opposite 'Birchwood', then R again

11 After 300 m (yd), on sharp RH bend just past letter box in the wall on the left bear L (in effect SA) 'Northleigh ¼'

12 Continue to end of tarmac. Leave all farm buildings to your left. Continue in same direction on stone track for 400 m (yd) as it climbs and swings to the right. At brow of hill, opposite gate on right L on grass/stone track

13 Fine descent. At fork halfway down bear L. At road L, then 1st R over bridge

14 Steep climb. At T-j with A39 L downhill

15 After 2½ km (1½ miles) 1st R 'Blakewell Fisheries'. After 800 m (½ mile) L onto No Through Road 'Blakewell Fisheries'

16 At end of tarmac SA onto rough track, which soon improves, by Higher Blackwell Farm

17 At X-roads SA 'Ashford, Heanton'. At next X-roads SA 'Ashford, Heanton'

18 After 400 m (¼ mile) 1st L 'Ashford', then at T-j just past church L 'Barnstaple' on Strand Lane

19 At T-j with main road (A361) R, then after 100 m (yd) by Strand House L onto Public Footpath, under bridge and up steps onto cycle path

20 Follow cycle path back to Barnstaple with the estuary on your right. With the football ground on the left and two 'Coastal Path' signs on a telegraph pole bear L away from water

21 At T-j with Pottington Road bear R onto Mill Road

22 At T-j with main road R. At roundabout R 'Library, Civic Centre, Sticklepath' to return to start

8 South from Lynton onto Exmoor

Start

Coombe Park Hotel
car park on the A39
east of Lynton

P As above

Distance and grade

29 km (18 miles)

Highly strenuous

Nearest railway

Barnstaple, 24 km
(15 miles) southwest
of Parracombe

A reasonably tough off-road ride, with over 760 m (2500 ft) of climbing and 10 valleys to cross. The views, the descents and the climbs are all memorable. For a ride that is never more than 3 km (2 miles) from the main A39, it has some surprisingly remote stretches. The ride starts with a steep climb from the hotel car park to Cheriton. This first valley, formed by the Hoaroak River (which joins the East Lyn River at Watersmeet), is a taste of things to come: a steep, at times technical, descent is followed by a steep climb, beginning with a section where you will need to push. The route makes use of yellow roads, white roads and bridleways to proceed westwards, more or less parallel with the A39 but a world away in atmosphere. Farmsteads at Radsbury, Thornworthy and Woolhanger, all high up on Exmoor, seem fairly remote, which is why the extraordinary music room at Woolhanger comes as a shock. The A39 is crossed just before Parracombe; this is your only chance for refuelling outside Lynton and Lynmouth. Soon after reaching the summit of Martinhoe Common, you descend through lovely woodland alongside a stream, emerging near Lee Bay with a breathtaking view of the coastline. 5 km (3 miles) of on-road riding lead you through The Valley of Rocks, with its amazing rock formations, into Lynton. Just when you thought you were close to the end, you are faced with the longest and toughest climb of the whole ride – nearly 300 m (1000 ft) from the Old Cottage Inn to West Lyn. (If this sounds too daunting you have the option of crossing from Lynton to Lynmouth and following the A39 for 5 km (3 miles) beside the river; there is a mere 192 m (630 ft) climb back to the hotel car park.)

Coombe Park Hotel | Cheriton | Thornworthy | Woolhanger | Churchtown | Parracombe | Bodley

Terrain

Lots of climbs: 131 m
(430 ft) from start to
Stock Common,
several 45 m (150 ft)
climbs across the
moor, 100 m (330 ft)
from Parracombe to
the A39, 100 m (330
ft) to Lee Abbey and
305 m (1000 ft) from
Lynton to the A39
above West Lyn

Refreshments

Fox and Goose PH 🍺, Parracombe
Lots of choice in Lynton
Rising Sun PH 🍺🍺, Lynmouth

Places of interest

Lynton *1*

Sited on a cliff 152 m (500 ft) above its sister village of Lynmouth, Lynton is protected from the worst of Exmoor's weather by a ring of hills. The Victorians realised this and developed the village as a seaside resort.

Lynmouth *1*

In 1812, the poet Shelley and his 16-year-old bride were captivated by the beautiful little village of Lynmouth. Since then, tourism has become its main staple, but the basic framework of towering cliffs and swirling river valleys remain. Disastrous floods caused by torrential rain in 1952 swept away part of the quay and killed 34 people.

The Valley of Rocks *22*

The poet Robert Southey described this area of jagged tors and breathtaking coastal scenery as 'rock reeling upon rock, stone piled upon stone, a huge terrific reeling mass'.

Martinhoe Common · Crosscombe Barton · Lee Abbey · The Valley of Rocks · Lynton · West Lyn

1 Exit car park and turn R over bridge. Steep climb. After 800 m (½ mile), by barn with wooden doors, as road swings sharply left downhill bear R (in effect SA) 'Cheriton'

2 Steep climb to Cheriton. Shortly after South Cheriton Farm B&B, follow road to the right, then after 50 m (yd) 2nd L 'Lyn Combe. Lyn Down'

3 Steep descent to river (ford/bridge) then steep climb the other side. Track becomes grassy once out of woodland

4 At four-way signpost SA 'Bridleway. Sparhanger Cross'. At T-j with road, on bend bear R (in effect SA), then after 200 m (yd) on sharp RH bend L 'Sparhanger Farm'

5 Steep descent. Cross ford. Steep climb. Surface turns from tarmac to loose stone. At T-j just beyond gate R 'Bridleway'

6 At T-j with road near 'Cattle Grid' sign L, then after 300 m (yd) 1st lane/track R by four-way signpost 'Public Bridleway. Martinhoe Cross A39 via Thornworthy and Woolhanger 2¼'

7 Follow steep, rocky track downhill to ford then up the other side. Through gateway at top of track 'Public Bridleway. Martinhoe Cross via Woolhanger 1¾'

8 The track soon peters out but bear slightly R and you will soon see the gate ahead through which the bridleway passes. Follow LH field-edge through gates, across a stream, past Woolhanger and onto tarmac

9 Just before joining A39 (busy main road) sharply L back on yourself on tarmac lane

10 At T-j after 1 km (¾ mile) L on No Through Road. After 100 m (yd) R onto track 'Bridleway to Parracombe'

11 Follow track past farm as it becomes narrower. Down stream bed to gate and bear R downhill

12 **Take care**. At A39 SA 'Bridleway. Parracombe'. Follow track as it turns to tarmac down into Parracombe village. At T-j with row of houses ahead L (or R for pub), then just after sharp LH bend by Parracombe School R 'Bodley, Lynton'

13 At X-roads at Bodley Cross SA 'Bodley' onto No Through Road. At end of tarmac R 'Bridleway via Newberry Lane'

14 Narrow track broadens. At tarmac SA past barn. At T-j by large lay-by with gravel R. At T-j with A39 at Killington Cross L 'Lynton'

15 **Easy to miss**. After 400 m (yd), just after LH bend, before the brow of the hill L through wooden gate into field 'Bridleway to Martinhoe Common. Kemacott'

16 Do not lose much height, head for gate opening between wall and hedgerow. You are aiming towards a hedgerow which runs uphill on the other side of the valley. Descend on obvious grassy track to cross stream, then take LH fork uphill

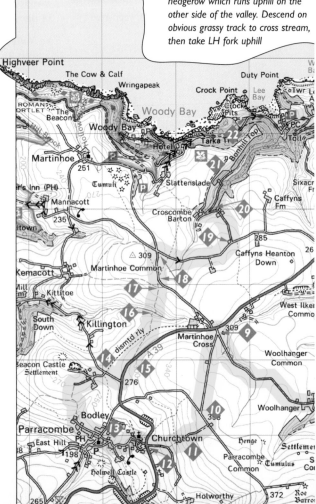

17 Climb LH field-edge. At gate R 'Bridleway to Martinhoe Common'

18 At road L. At T-j with road L. After 800 m (½ mile) at X-roads R 'Caffyns. Lynton'

19 After 800 m (½ mile) at black, corrugated-iron barn L onto tarmac lane 'Croscombe Barton. Bridleway only to Crock Pits'

20 At bottom of hill by large, lovely stone house **stop**! Turn R sharply back on yourself 'Crock Pits 1. Lynton 2¼'

21 There are several tracks in the wood, so instructions are somewhat difficult. The river is crossed once, then you keep the river to your right

and contour gently downhill. Follow river on good broad track (bridleway signs for 'Crock Pits') keeping to lower track, then at fork bear L onto upper track following signs for 'Woody Bay 1¾. County Road ¼'

22 At T-j with road R (fabulous sea views). Fast descent then steep climb through the Valley of Rocks

23 Through Lynton. At 'STOP' sign SA onto B3234 'Barnstaple (A39)', then after 800 m (½ mile) L by Old Cottage Inn PH

24 Cross bridge, turn L then immediately R 'Summerhouse Hill via West Lyn'

25 If in doubt, take the steepest option on this tough push. At farm SA 'Hillsford Bridge. Brendon'

26 At X-roads with A39 L 'Lynmouth. Brendon. Simonsbath'

27 After a mile, on sharp LH hairpin bend R 'Simonsbath B3223', then immediately R 'Bridge Ball. Cheriton' and R again to return to start

In and out of the Sid valley east of Ottery St Mary

East of Ottery St Mary and the valley of the River Otter lies a compact range of wooded hills that rises to 244 m (800 ft). The River Sid and its tributaries cut through this range, giving rise to some very fine views and steep hills. A flat 3 km (2 miles) road section north from Ottery St Mary gives you a chance to warm up before the first of the steep climbs – 183 m (600 ft) from Alfington to Putts Corner. The climb starts gently, becomes very steep and then the gradient eases again. You pass through beautiful woodland to arrive on top of the ridge, just north of the source of the Sid. A fast descent beside a stream takes you to a side valley. Parts of the next hill seem even steeper than the first as you climb to the top of the ridge. This is followed southwest on tarmac and track for 3 km (2 miles) before a steep, tunnel-like descent through a pine forest takes you to the road. The middle section of the ride is on tarmac and passes through Sidmouth, giving you the opportunity for refreshment before the last and longest climb up Core Hill and Beacon Hill. The top section of this climb is a real delight – good, broad, stone-based tracks through broad-leaf woodland. Although you are now on a ridge, you will only appreciate this if you turn off the road into the car park on the left where the views open out over the Otter valley. A descent on track, then tarmac takes you past the lovely house of Knightstone and to the last off-road mile back to Ottery St Mary.

Start

The Volunteer Inn, the Square, Ottery St Mary

P Long-stay car park on road towards Talaton

Distance and grade

29 km (18 miles)

Strenuous

Terrain

Three main climbs, all very steep at some stage: 183 m (600 ft) from Alfington to Putts Corner, 91 m (300 ft) from Lower Mincombe Farm onto the next ridge and 228 m (750 ft) from Sidmouth to White Cross

Nearest railway

Honiton, 6½ km (4 miles) north of Farway Hill

Ottery St Mary

Alfington

Westgate Hill

Putts Corner

Lower Knapp Farm

Lower Mincombe Farm

Buckton

Places of interest

Ottery St Mary 1

Various literary figures are associated with this town: Samuel Taylor Coleridge was born here in 1772 and William Thackeray set his novel *Pendennis* here (the name was changed to Clavering St Mary). The magnificent collegiate church dates from 1337. Notable features include an Elizabethan clock and a minstrels' gallery.

Refreshments

Lots of choice in Ottery St Mary
Alfington Inn PH, Alfington
Hare and Hounds PH, Putts Corner
Lots of choice in Sidmouth

Cadhay House, near Ottery St Mary 1

Cadhay House was built in 1550 on the site of an earlier house; the new house incorporated the original Great Hall with its fine timbered roof.

Sidmouth 13/14

An ancient fishing port, Sidmouth developed as a seaside resort in Georgian times.

Sidmouth

Sidmouth   Beacon Hill   East Hill   Knightstone

1 With back to the Volunteer Inn diagonally R onto Silver Street 'Honiton, Otter Nurseries, Tourist Information Centre'

2 After almost 3 km (2 miles), in Alfington, 100 m (yd) after a filling station/stores on the right but 50 m (yd) **before** the Alfington Inn PH on the left, R 'Public Bridleway'

3 Gentle then steep climb. At T-j with road R

4 At T-j with B3174 L 'Sidmouth 5, Seaton 8'

5 At X-roads with A375 at Putts Corner by Hare and Hounds PH SA 'Seaton, Lyme Regis'

6 After 1 km (¾ mile), at 1st house on the right ('Shepherds Croft') R over cattle grid 'Middle Knapp Farm'. After 100 m (yd) 1st L through metal gates (blue arrow)

7 Very steep tarmac descent then stony/grassy track alongside stream. Through gate and L through farm continuing in same direction down the valley on a concrete track

8 At road R, then after 300 m (yd), opposite 1st farm on the right L through metal gate onto track 'Public Bridleway'

9 Very steep climb on good stony track. At road R for 2½ km (1½ miles) passing Sweetcombe Heights and two tarmac turns on the left. As road starts to descend, take the first stony track on L 'Public Bridleway'

10 Follow in same direction as it changes from a broad, stony track to a narrow, rough track for 200 m (yd). On a sharp RH bend bear L (faint yellow mark on tree). This stretch might be muddy

11 Very steep, wooded descent. The last 100 m (yd) might be overgrown. Emerge in field and head SA towards the telegraph pole in the bottom corner

12 Through gate and SA downhill on road. After 50 m (yd), as road turns sharp right bear L (in effect SA) onto broad stony track. At road SA downhill

13 At X-roads with A3052 at Stevens Cross SA 'Fortescue ½, Sidmouth 1½'. After 2 km (1¼ miles), shortly after the road emerges into the open, by Sid Cottage and a letter box set into the wall on the right, take the 1st signposted R on Sid Lane

14 Cross river via bridge and SA uphill on the other side. At T-j at end of Sid Park Road R, then 3rd L on sharp RH bend onto Arcot Road 'Exeter'

15 Go past Balfour Arms PH and church. Just after bus shelter on right, opposite letter box in wall R up Core Hill Road

16 At X-roads with two main roads SA. Tarmac then stone track on a long climb. Lovely section through woodland at the top

17 At junction of roads at White Cross SA 'East Hill Strip ¼, Ottery St Mary 4'

18 After 800 m (½ mile), you will come to a picnic site car park on the left. It is worth diverting via the car park for the fine views. After rejoining the road, ignore the 1st left (wooden gate and fence), take the next L after 300 m (yd) (no gate)

19 Steep downhill. At X-roads with tarmac SA. After 1 km (¾ mile), just after a turning to the left R between stone pillars by the fine old house of Knightstone

20 At times rough. At T-j with tarmac L, then at T-j at end of Slade Road L. At T-j at end of Jesu Street R to return to start

Notes

Notes

Useful addresses

British Cycling Federation
National Cycling Centre
Stuart Street
Manchester M11 4DQ
0870 871 2000
www.bcf.uk.com

The BCF co-ordinates and promotes an array of cycle sports and cycling in general. They are a good first point of contact if you want to find out more about how to get involved in cycling. The website provides information on upcoming cycle events and competitions.

CTC (Cyclists Touring Club)
Cotterell House
69 Meadrow
Godalming
Surrey GU7 3HS
01483 417217
www.ctc.org.uk

Britain's largest cycling organisation, promoting recreational and utility cycling. The CTC provides touring and technical advice, legal aid and insurance, and campaigns to improve facilities and opportunities for all cyclists. The website provides details of campaigns and routes and has an online application form.

The London Cycling Campaign
Unit 228
30 Great Guildford Street
London SE1 0HS
020 7928 7220
www.lcc.org.uk

The LCC promotes cycling in London by providing services for cyclists and by campaigning for more facilities for cyclists. Membership of the LCC provides the following benefits: London Cyclist magazine, insurance, legal advice, workshops, organised rides, discounts in bike shops and much more. You can join the LCC on its website.

Sustrans
Head Office
Crown House
37-41 Prince Street
Bristol BS1 4PS
General information line: 0117 929 0888
www.sustrans.org.uk

A registered charity, Sustrans designs and builds systems for sustainable transport. It is best known for its transformation of old railway lines into safe, traffic-free routes for cyclists and pedestrians and wheelchair users. Sustrans is developing the 13,000 km (8000 mile) National Cycle Network on traffic-calmed minor roads and traffic-free paths, to be completed by the year 2005 with major funding from the Millennium Commission.

Veteran Cycle Club
Membership Secretary
31 Yorke Road
Croxley Green
Rickmansworth
Herts WD3 3DW
www.v-cc.org.uk

A very active club, the VCC is concerned with the history and restoration of veteran cycles. Members enjoy organised rides and receive excellent publications relating to cycle history and club news.